Algebra Skills Edexcel Maths Higher GCSE 9-1

T0315977

Revision & Practice

GCSE 9-1

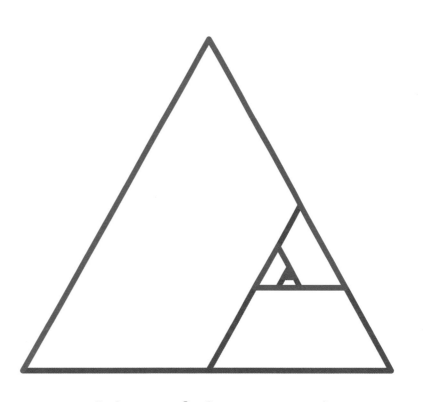

Build confidence with targeted skills practice

First published in the UK by Scholastic, 2017; this edition published 2024

Scholastic Distribution Centre, Bosworth Avenue, Tournament Fields, Warwick CV34 6UQ

Scholastic Ireland, 89E Lagan Road, Dublin Industrial Estate, Glasnevin, Dublin D11 HP5F

www.scholastic.co.uk

SCHOLASTIC and associated logos are trademarks and/or registered trademarks of Scholastic Inc.
© Scholastic 2017, 2024

1 2 3 4 5 6 7 8 9   4 5 6 7 8 9 0 1 2 3

A CIP catalogue record for this book is available from the British Library.
ISBN 978-0702-33235-7
Printed by Leo Paper Products, China

The book is made of materials from well-managed, FSC®-certified forests and other controlled sources.
All rights reserved.

This book is sold subject to the condition that it shall not, by way of trade or otherwise, be lent, hired out or otherwise circulated in any form of binding or cover other than that in which it is published. No part of this publication may be reproduced, stored in a retrieval system, or transmitted, in any form or by any means, electronic, mechanical, photocopying, recording or otherwise, other than for the purposes described in the content of this product, without prior written permission of Scholastic.

Due to the nature of the web, we cannot guarantee the content or links of any site mentioned.

Every effort has been made to trace copyright holders for the works reproduced in this book, and the publishers apologise for any inadvertent omissions.

Author Stephen Doyle

Editorial team Rachel Morgan, Audrey Stokes, Julia Roberts, Haremi Ltd

Series designers emc design ltd

Typesetting York Publishing Solutions Pvt. Ltd. & QBS Learning

Illustrations York Publishing Solutions Pvt. Ltd.

Cover illustration Golden Ratio, david.costa.art/Shutterstock

Notes from the publisher

Please use this product in conjunction with the official specification and sample assessment materials. Ask your teacher if you are unsure where to find them.

The marks and star ratings have been suggested by our subject experts, but they are to be used as a guide only.

Answer space has been provided, but you may need to use additional paper for your workings.

Contents

How to use this book

Inside this book you'll find everything you need to boost your skills in Algebra to help you succeed in the GCSE 9–1 Edexcel Higher Mathematics specification. It combines revision and exam practice in one handy solution. Work through the revision material first or dip into the exam practice section as you complete each subtopic. This book will focus on algebra but within your revision you will of course include other topics to ensure overall success. This book gives you the flexibility to revise your way!

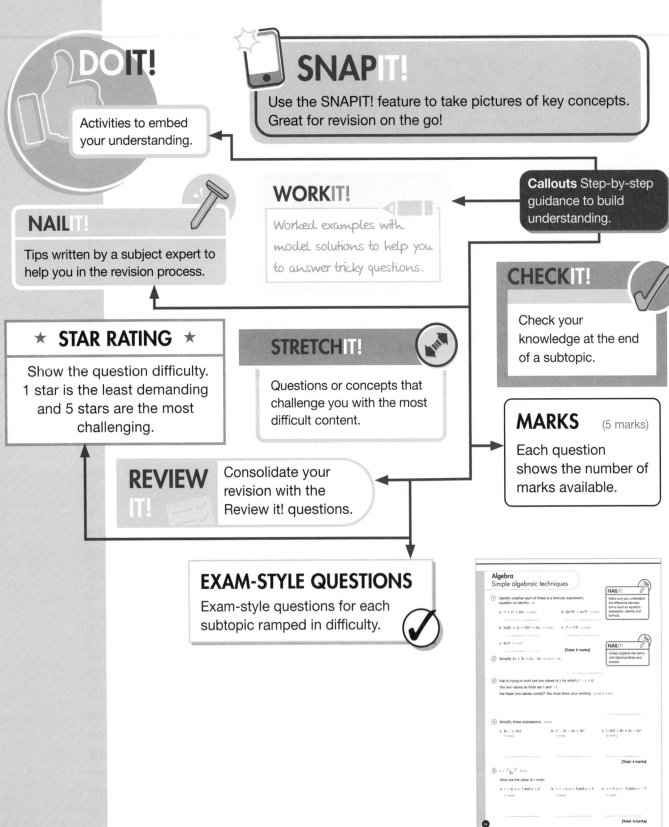

DOIT!
Activities to embed your understanding.

SNAPIT!
Use the SNAPIT! feature to take pictures of key concepts. Great for revision on the go!

WORKIT!
Worked examples with model solutions to help you to answer tricky questions.

Callouts Step-by-step guidance to build understanding.

NAILIT!
Tips written by a subject expert to help you in the revision process.

CHECKIT!
Check your knowledge at the end of a subtopic.

★ STAR RATING ★
Show the question difficulty. 1 star is the least demanding and 5 stars are the most challenging.

STRETCHIT!
Questions or concepts that challenge you with the most difficult content.

MARKS (5 marks)
Each question shows the number of marks available.

REVIEW IT!
Consolidate your revision with the Review it! questions.

EXAM-STYLE QUESTIONS
Exam-style questions for each subtopic ramped in difficulty.

REVISION

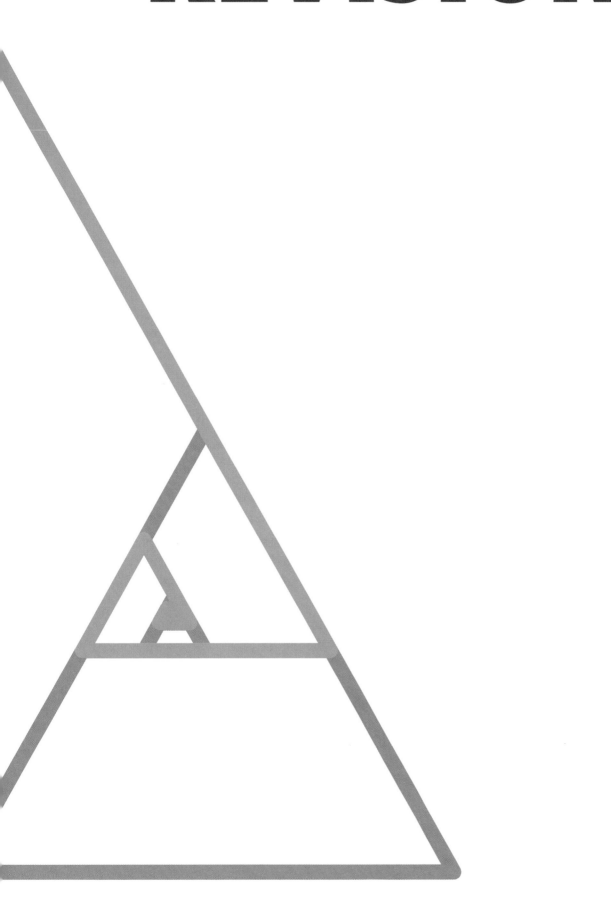

Algebra

Simple algebraic techniques

There are conventions (rules that everyone follows) when using algebra.

SNAP IT! Algebraic conventions

Write:

- ab instead of $a \times b$
- $3a$ instead of $a + a + a$ and $3 \times a$

- b^2 instead of $b \times b$
- a^3 instead of $a \times a \times a$
- a^2b instead of $a \times a \times b$

- $\frac{a}{b}$ instead of $a \div b$
- $\frac{1}{2}x$ or $\frac{x}{2}$ instead of $x \div 2$

Words used in maths

When using algebra certain words are used. Here are the ones you need to know about.

SNAP IT! Algebra terms

Equations contain letters and/or numbers and they always contain an equals sign. Examples include $2x + 4 = 2$, $3x - 4 = x + 6$, $x^2 + 2x + 1 = 0$.

Expressions contain letters and/or numbers but there is no equals sign. Examples include $2x - y^2$, $(x + 3)(x - 2)$.

Identities are true for all values of the letter or letters.

Examples include $(x + 1)^2 \equiv x^2 + 2x + 1$ or $(x - 2)^2 \equiv x^2 - 4x + 4$.

Formulae contain letters and/or words to represent variable quantities (**variables**) and they also contain an equals sign.

Terms are a single number or variable, or numbers and variables multiplied together. Terms are always separated by $+$ or $-$ signs. In the expression $5ab - 2a + 4$, $5ab$, $-2a$ and 4 are all terms.

Factors are what you can multiply together to get an expression in algebra. For example, $2x(x + 3) = 2x^2 + 6x$ so $2x$ and $(x + 3)$ are both factors of $2x^2 + 6x$.

> The symbol $\equiv$ means 'is equivalent to'.
>
> Notice that the left-hand side is identical to the right-hand side, so this could not be solved like an equation.

Collecting like terms

Like terms are terms that have identical letters and powers. To simplify an expression you can collect like terms (find the sum of them). For example, $4x^2y$ can be combined with $-14x^2y$, but it cannot be combined with $-2xy^2$ or $5xy$.

WORKIT!

> Rearrange with the like terms grouped together.

Simplify these expressions.

a $4x^2 + 6x - x + 6x^2 + 3$

$4x^2 + 6x - x + 6x^2 + 3 = 4x^2 + 6x^2 + 6x - x + 3$
$= 10x^2 + 5x + 3$

b $6a - b - c + a - 4a + c$

$6a - b - c + a - 4a + c = 6a + a - 4a - b - c + c = 3a - b$

c $4yx + x^2 + 6xy - 4x^2$

$4yx + x^2 + 6xy - 4x^2 = 4xy + 6xy + x^2 - 4x^2 = 10xy - 3x^2$

> Always give answers in descending powers (e.g. x^3, then x^2, then x and finally ordinary numbers (e.g. 2)).

> Always look at both the sign and the value of a letter or number

> Although the order of the letters in a term does not matter ($4yx$ is the same as $4xy$), the convention is to write the number and then the letters in alphabetical order.

Substituting numerical values into formulae and expressions

This is the sort of calculation you often do in other subjects such as physics and chemistry. Replace each letter in the formula or expression with the numerical value given in the question and calculate.

WORKIT!

In the formula $p = \frac{nRT}{v}$, find the value of p if $n = 5$, $R = 8.31$, $v = 3$ and $T = 298$. Give your answer to 3 significant figures.

$p = \dfrac{nRT}{v} = \dfrac{5 \times 8.31 \times 298}{3}$

$= 4127.3$

$= 4130$ (to 3 s.f.)

> Write the equation and replace each letter by its value.

> Always check the question to see how many decimal places or significant figures should be used.

WORKIT!

Find the value of $b^2 - 4ac$ when $a = -1$, $b = -5$ and $c = 4$.

$b^2 - 4ac = (-5)^2 - 4(-1)(4)$

$= 25 + 16 = 41$

> Notice the use of BIDMAS.

DOIT!

Write an example of an equation, expression, etc. on different cards. Write the terms on another set of cards. Practise matching the cards.

NAILIT!

It is a good idea to add brackets around minus values in order to emphasise them.

✓ CHECKIT!

1 Identify whether each of the following is a formula, expression, equation or identity.

a $s = ut + \frac{1}{2}at^2$

d $(x^2y)^3 = x^6y^3$

b $2(x^2 + y^2) = 2x^2 + 2y^2$

e $2x + 1 = 3$

c $4x^3y^2$

2 Simplify

a $15x^2 - 4x + x^2 + 9x - x - 6x^2$

b $7a + 5b - b - 4a - 5b$

c $8yx + 5x^2 + 2xy - 8x^2$

d $x^3 + 3x - 5 + 2x^3 - 4x$

3 If $P = I^2R$, find P when $I = \frac{2}{3}$ and $R = 36$.

4 Using $v = u + at$, find v when $u = 20$, $a = -8$ and $t = 2$.

Removing brackets

Multiplying out a single bracket

Multiply each term inside the bracket by the term outside the brackets. Be careful when there is a negative outside the bracket as it will change the signs of all the terms inside the bracket.

WORKIT!

Multiply out the brackets and simplify your answer.

a $3(2x + 4)$

> Multiply each term in the bracket by the number outside the bracket.

$3 \times 2x + 3 \times 4 = 6x + 12$

b $-6(x - 1)$

$-6 \times x + (-6) \times (-1) = -6x + 6$

> The minus sign changes the sign of every term inside the bracket.

c $5(2x - 3) + 4(x - 1)$

$5 \times 2x + 5 \times (-3) + 4 \times x + 4 \times (-1)$
$= 10x - 15 + 4x - 4$
$= 14x - 19$

> Multiply out the brackets, then collect like terms.

d $-(4 - x)$

> $-(4 - x)$ is the same as $-1 \times (4 - x)$.

$-4 + x = x - 4$

Using the laws of indices with brackets

When multiplying out brackets you may have to use the laws of indices. A useful law is $x^a \times x^b = x^{a+b}$ so for example $x^3 \times x^2 = x^{3+2} = x^5$.

WORKIT!

Expand and simplify

a $2x(3x + 7)$

$2x \times 3x + 2x \times 7 = 6x^2 + 14x$

> Remember that $x = x^1$.

b $4a(2a^2 - 3a + 4)$

$4a \times 2a^2 + 4a \times (-3a) + 4a \times 4 = 8a^3 - 12a^2 + 16a$

c $5x^2y^3z(3x + 7yz)$

$5x^2y^3z \times 3x + 5x^2y^3z \times 7yz = 15x^3y^3z + 35x^2y^4z^2$

Multiplying brackets

When multiplying pairs of brackets, all the terms in the first bracket must be multiplied by all the terms in the second bracket. There are different methods you can use to multiply two pairs of brackets together.

Method 1: the 'face' method

Using the 'face' method, the curved lines show that all the terms are multiplied together.

$(x + 2) \ (x - 3)$

Start from the top first and work from left to right:

- multiply x by x to give x^2

- multiply $+2$ by -3 to give -6

- multiply x by -3 to give $-3x$ ◄— Now go to the bottom curved lines.

- multiply $+2$ by x to give $+2x$.

So, $(x + 2)(x - 3) = x^2 - 6 - 3x + 2x$
$= x^2 - x - 6.$ ◄— Notice that the answer is given in descending powers of x.

Method 2

Each term in the first bracket multiplies the contents of the second bracket:

$(x + 2)(x - 3) = x(x - 3) + 2(x - 3)$

$= x^2 - 3x + 2x - 6$ ◄— Multiply out each bracket.

$= x^2 - x - 6$ ◄— Simplify by collecting terms in x.

We will use Method 2 in this book, but you should use the method you are happiest with.

The curved lines look like a face (eyebrows, nose and mouth) and remind you what to multiply.

NAILIT!

Try both methods and use the one you find easier.

NAILIT!

With practice, you may find that you do not need to write the first step, but can go straight to multiplying out each bracket.

WORKIT!

Expand ◄— 'Expand' means 'multiply out'.

a $(x + 5)(x - 2)$

$x(x - 2) + 5(x - 2) = x^2 - 2x + 5x - 10$

$= x^2 + 3x - 10$ ◄— Collect like terms in x.

b $(2x - 7)(4x - 2)$

$2x(4x - 2) - 7(4x - 2) = 8x^2 - 4x - 28x + 14$ ◄— Remember to keep the sign with the second term from the first bracket. You need to multiply each term in the second bracket by -7.

$= 8x^2 - 32x + 14$

c $(a + b)^2$

$a(a + b) + b(a + b) = a^2 + ab + ab + b^2$

$= a^2 + 2ab + b^2$

$(a + b)^2$ means $(a + b)(a + b)$.

To expand an expression containing three sets of brackets, expand the first pair of brackets. Then expand this expression with the third bracket.

WORKIT!

Expand $(2x - 1)(x + 5)(3x - 2)$.

> It is acceptable to use 1s in your working out.

$[2x(x + 5) - 1(x + 5)](3x - 2)$

> First expand $(2x - 1)(x + 5)$.

$= (2x^2 + 10x - x - 5)(3x - 2)$

$= (2x^2 + 9x - 5)(3x - 2)$

$= 2x^2(3x - 2) + 9x(3x - 2) - 5(3x - 2)$

> Multiply each term in $2x^2 + 9x - 5$ by each term in $3x - 2$.

$= 6x^3 - 4x^2 + 27x^2 - 18x - 15x + 10$

$= 6x^3 + 23x^2 - 33x + 10$

DOIT!

Write out the expansion of two brackets and make notes or write instructions beside each line of your working.

CHECKIT!

1 Multiply out

  a $2(x + 4)$ **d** $x(3x - 1)$

  b $7(9x + 3)$ **e** $3x(x + 1)$

  c $-(1 - x)$ **f** $4x(5x - 2)$

2 Multiply out and simplify

  a $2(x + 3) + 3(x + 2)$

  b $6(x + 4) - 3(x - 7)$

  c $x(3x + 1) + x(x + 1)$

  d $x(3x - 4) - 2(3x - 4)$

3 Expand and simplify

  a $(t + 3)(t + 5)$

  b $(x - 3)(x + 3)$

  c $(2y + 9)(3y + 7)$

  d $(2x - 1)^2$

4 Expand and simplify

  a $(x + 7)(x + 2)(2x + 3)$

  b $(2x - 1)(3x - 2)(4x - 3)$

Factorising

Factorisation is the opposite process to expanding brackets.

Factorising a simple expression

Any factors that are common to all terms in an expression can be taken outside a bracket. These may be letters or numbers. When the terms include numbers (**coefficients**) the highest common factor of these is taken outside.

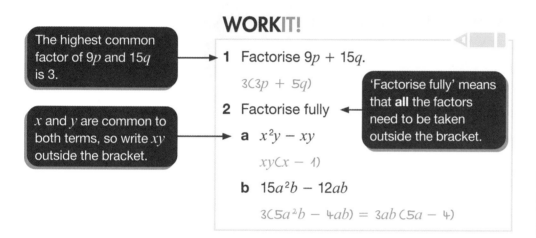

WORKIT!

The highest common factor of $9p$ and $15q$ is 3.

1 Factorise $9p + 15q$.

$3(3p + 5q)$

'Factorise fully' means that **all** the factors need to be taken outside the bracket.

x and y are common to both terms, so write xy outside the bracket.

2 Factorise fully

a $x^2y - xy$

$xy(x - 1)$

b $15a^2b - 12ab$

$3(5a^2b - 4ab) = 3ab(5a - 4)$

Factorising a quadratic expression

Factorising a quadratic expression gives two linear expressions in brackets. For example, $x^2 - 3x + 2$ factorises to $(x - 1)(x - 2)$.

> Linear expressions contain the variable to the power 1 and no higher: for example, $2x - 7$.

There are many different methods for factorising a quadratic expression, one of which is shown below. This method is particularly useful when the numbers in the quadratic expression are large.

Suppose you are asked to factorise $x^2 + 7x - 30$.

You need to find two factors that multiply together to give -30. They also need to add together to give the coefficient of x ($+7$ in this case).

> The coefficient of x is the number in front of x.

State the factor pairs of -30:

1 and -30	3 and -10	6 and -5
-1 and 30	-3 and 10	-6 and 5

Then look for the pair of numbers in the above list that add together to give 7:

-3 and 10.

With practice you may not need to write the list out.

Now write the two factors you have found as the coefficients of the x terms like this:

$x^2 + 7x - 30 = x^2 - 3x + 10x - 30$

Then factorise the first two terms by taking a term in x out and also the last two terms by taking a number out like this:

$x^2 - 3x + 10x - 30 = x(x - 3) + 10(x - 3)$

The term $(x - 3)$ is common, so may be taken out as a factor in the following way:

$x(x - 3) + 10(x - 3) = (x - 3)(x + 10)$

This may seem long-winded, but it works with all quadratic expressions that can be factorised, as the following examples show.

> The terms inside the brackets have to be identical.

> If you had written the factors the other way round it would still work:
> $x^2 + 10x - 3x - 30$
> $= x(x + 10) - 3(x + 10)$
> $= (x + 10)(x - 3)$.

WORKIT!

Factorise $x^2 - 9x + 18$.

$x^2 - 9x + 18 = x^2 - 6x - 3x + 18$

$= x(x - 6) - 3(x - 6)$

$= (x - 6)(x - 3)$

> The factors of 18 that add together to give -9 are -6 and -3. These are written as the coefficients of both x-terms.

> The coefficient of x^2 is the number in front of x^2.

If the coefficient of x^2 is not 1, multiply it by the number term. Then look for factor pairs of this number.

WORKIT!

Factorise $6x^2 - 17x + 12$.

$6x^2 - 17x + 12 = 6x^2 - 9x - 8x + 12$

$= 3x(2x - 3) - 4(2x - 3)$

$= (2x - 3)(3x - 4)$

> $6 \times 12 = 72$
> Look for a factor pair of 72 that adds to give -17: -9 and -8.

> Notice that the sign for the number outside the bracket is negative. This makes the contents of both brackets identical.

The difference of two squares

A perfect square is a number or expression whose square root does not contain a square root symbol. For example, 16, $36a^2$ and $100x^2y^4$ are all perfect squares; 10, $16b^3$ and $9xy^2$ are not perfect squares.

If two terms are both perfect squares with a minus sign between them, such as $x^2 - y^2$, this is called the difference of two squares. They can be factorised like this: $x^2 - y^2 = (x + y)(x - y)$.

Both terms must be perfect squares, so capable of being easily square rooted. Note that this only works when there is a minus sign between the two terms. For example:

$4x^2 - 9y^2 = (2x + 3y)(2x - 3y)$

$16x^2 - 25 = (4x + 5)(4x - 5)$

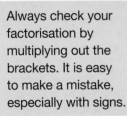

NAILIT!

Always check your factorisation by multiplying out the brackets. It is easy to make a mistake, especially with signs.

> Square root each term and put them in brackets: one bracket has a + sign between the terms and the other has a − sign.

SNAPIT!

Difference of two squares

Learn the formula for the difference of two squares:

$a^2 - b^2 \equiv (a + b)(a - b)$

Factorising to simplify

Sometimes the question does not state that you need to factorise, but it is necessary in order to simplify an expression.

WORKIT!

Show that $\frac{1}{9x^2-1} \div \frac{1}{3x^2+20x-7}$ simplifies to $\frac{ax+b}{cx+d}$ where a, b, c and d are integers.

$$\frac{1}{9x^2-1} \div \frac{1}{3x^2+20x-7} = \frac{3x^2+20x-7}{9x^2-1}$$

Express the division as a single fraction.

$$= \frac{(3x-1)(x+7)}{(3x+1)(3x-1)}$$

Factorise both the numerator and the denominator.

$$= \frac{x+7}{3x+1}$$

Cancel the common factor.

DOIT!

Write a quick summary of how to factorise algebraic expressions.

✓ CHECKIT!

1 Factorise fully

  a $24t + 18$

  b $9a - 2ab$

  c $5xy + 15yz$

  d $24x^3y^2 + 6xy^2$

2 Factorise

  a $x^2 + 10x + 21$

  b $x^2 + 2x - 15$

  c $6x^2 + 19x + 10$

  d $4x^2 - 49$

3 Work out

$$\frac{1}{x-7} - \frac{x+10}{2x^2-11x-21}$$

Express your answer in its simplest form.

Changing the subject of a formula

Changing the subject of a formula helps you to find a particular quantity. You need to get the letter representing that quantity on the left of the equals sign and everything else on the right. For example:

$$n = \frac{m}{M}$$

> The upper case and lower case letters mean different things, so they are separate terms.

As n is on its own on the left-hand side, it is the **subject** of the formula. To change the subject of the formula to m, you need to remove M from the right-hand side. Multiply both sides by M to give:

> We normally write the letters in an equation in alphabetical order: Mn rather than nM.

$$Mn = \frac{Mm}{M}$$

Cancel the M in the top and bottom of the fraction on the right-hand side:

$$Mn = m$$

Swap this around to give:

> m is now the subject.

$$m = Mn$$

To make M the subject of $n = \frac{m}{M}$, first multiply both sides by M to give:

$$Mn = m$$

Then remove the n from the left-hand side by dividing both sides by n.

> M is now the subject.

So, $M = \frac{m}{n}$

WORKIT!

Rearrange the following equations to make the bracketed letter the subject of the formula.

a $y = \frac{1}{x}$ (x)

> Multiply both sides by x to remove x from the denominator.

$$xy = 1$$

> Divide both sides by y.

$$x = \frac{1}{y}$$

b $y = 2x + 6$ (x)

> Subtract 6 from both sides.

$$y - 6 = 2x$$

> Divide both sides by 2.

$$x = \frac{y - 6}{2}$$

c $r^2 = a^2 + b^2$ (b)

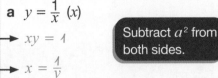
Subtract a^2 from both sides.

$$r^2 - a^2 = b^2$$

$$b^2 = r^2 - a^2$$

$$b = \sqrt{r^2 - a^2}$$

> Square root both sides.

NAILIT!

Always put the subject of the formula on the left-hand side.

Rearranging a formula for a term that appears on both sides

SNAPIT!   Rearranging formulae

When the new subject appears on both sides of a formula:

1. If there are any brackets, multiply them out.

2. Get all the terms that contain the subject on one side of the equation and all the other terms on the other side.

3. Take the new subject out as a factor so you will have it multiplied by the contents of a bracket.

4. Divide both sides by the bracket, leaving the subject on its own on the left of the equation.

WORKIT!

Make y the subject of the formula $3(3x - y) = 9 - 4xy$.

Collect the terms containing the new subject on one side and all the other terms on the other side.

$$9x - 3y = 9 - 4xy$$

Multiply out the brackets.

$$4xy - 3y = 9 - 9x$$

$$y(4x - 3) = 9 - 9x$$

Take the new subject, y, out of a bracket as a factor.

Divide both sides by the contents of the bracket to leave the new subject on its own.

$$y = \frac{9 - 9x}{4x - 3}$$

DOIT!

Draw a flowchart for rearranging a formula when the subject appears on both sides.

CHECKIT!

1 Make r the subject of the formula.

a $A = \pi r^2$

b $A = 4\pi r^2$

c $V = \frac{4}{3}\pi r^3$

2 Make the bracketed symbol the subject of the formula.

a $y = mx + c$ (c)

b $v = u + at$ (u)

c $v = u + at$ (a)

d $v^2 = 2as$ (s)

e $v^2 = u^2 + 2as$ (u)

f $s = \frac{1}{2}(u + v)t$ (t)

Solving linear equations

Linear equations are ones where the unknown or **variable** doesn't have a power (except 1). The variable is usually called x, but it can be any letter or symbol. You only need one linear equation to solve one variable.

Remember that an equation is like a balance. If you apply a process to one side (such as add a number), then for the equation to remain in balance, the same process (adding the same number) must be applied to the other side.

NAIL IT!

Remember:
$x = x^1$

WORKIT!

Solve these equations.

a $x + 5 = 7$

$x + 5 - 5 = 7 - 5$

$x = 2$

b $4x = 24$

$x = 24 \div 4 = 6$

c $4x - 7 = 21$

$4x = 28$

$x = 7$

d $\frac{2x - 7}{3} = 7$

$2x - 7 = 21$

$2x = 28$

$x = 14$

> You want to get x on its own on the left-hand side.
> Subtract 5 from both sides.

> To remove the 4 in front of the x, divide both sides by 4.

> Remove the denominator by multiplying both sides by 3.

> First, get a term in x on its own. Add 7 to both sides.

Linear equations involving brackets

When solving linear equations containing brackets, first multiply out the brackets and collect any like terms. Then solve the equation in the way outlined in the previous examples.

WORKIT!

Solve these equations.

a $4(2x - 3) = 4$

$8x - 12 = 4$

$8x = 16$

$x = 2$

b $5(x - 3) - 3(x + 1) = 0$

$5x - 15 - 3x - 3 = 0$

$2x - 18 = 0$

$2x = 18$

$x = 9$

> Multiply out the brackets.

> Multiply out the brackets and collect like terms.

NAIL IT!

It is better to rearrange the equation in such a way that the unknown quantity is positive.

Unknown quantity on both sides of the equation

If the unknown quantity (i.e. the quantity you are asked to find) appears on both sides of the equation, you must get it on just one side.

WORKIT!

Solve these equations.

a $2x - 1 = x + 4$

$x - 1 = 4$

$x = 5$

> You could subtract $2x$ from both sides but this would give $-x$ on the right-hand side. Subtracting x from both sides is a better option.

b $3(3x - 5) = 12(x - 7)$

$9x - 15 = 12x - 84$

$-15 = 3x - 84$

$69 = 3x$

$23 = x$

$x = 23$

> Subtract $9x$ from both sides.

> Add 84 to both sides.

NAILIT!

Solving linear equations is very important in GCSE mathematics as it happens in different kinds of questions. It is essential that you master all the techniques here as they will be needed elsewhere.

DOIT!

Make up some linear equations.
Solve them tomorrow. Are your answers all integers?

CHECKIT!

1 Solve these equations.

a $x - 7 = -4$ **c** $\frac{x}{5} = 4$

b $9x = 27$

2 Solve these equations.

a $3x + 1 = 16$ **c** $\frac{3x}{5} + 4 = 16$

b $\frac{2x}{3} = 12$

3 Solve these equations.

a $5(1 - x) = 15$

b $2m - 4 = m - 3$

c $9(4x - 3) = 3(2x + 3)$

Solving quadratic equations using factorisation

A quadratic equation is an equation that can be expressed in the form:

$ax^2 + bx + c = 0$

where a, b and c are numbers.

To solve a quadratic using factorisation, first put the equation into the form above and then factorise it. For example, to solve $2x^2 = 5 - 9x$, first rearrange it as $2x^2 + 9x - 5 = 0$ and then factorise it to give:

$(2x - 1)(x + 5) = 0$

For this to equal zero, one of the brackets must equal zero:

Hence $2x - 1 = 0$ or $x + 5 = 0$,

giving $x = \dfrac{1}{2}$ or $x = -5$

> Before factorising, the quadratic expression must be equal to zero.

NAIL IT!

You need to be able to solve simple linear equations to solve quadratic equations by factorisation.

WORKIT!

Solve $2x^2 + 7x - 4 = 0$

$(2x - 1)(x + 4) = 0$ ◄———— | Factorise $2x^2 + 7x - 4$.

$2x - 1 = 0$ or $x + 4 = 0$ ◄———— | Put each bracket equal to 0.

$x = \dfrac{1}{2}$ or $x = -4$

WORKIT!

This rectangle has an area of 60. Find the value of x.

Area of rectangle $=$ length $\times$ width

$\qquad\qquad\quad = 6x(2x + 1)$

> Substitute area = 60.

$60 = 6x(2x + 1)$

$60 = 12x^2 + 6x$

$0 = 12x^2 + 6x - 60$

$12x^2 + 6x - 60 = 0$ ◄———— | Divide both sides by 6 to make the factorisation easier.

$2x^2 + x - 10 = 0$

$(2x + 5)(x - 2) = 0$

$x = -\dfrac{5}{2}$ or $x = 2$ ◄———— | Put each bracket equal to 0 and solve.

$x = -\dfrac{5}{2}$ would give a length of $6 \times \left(-\dfrac{5}{2}\right) = -15$, which is impossible.

$\qquad$ So $x = 2$

(rectangle labelled $6x$ across top and $2x + 1$ down the right side)

NAIL IT!

Always check to see if both values are possible or only one of them. In some situations, you can ignore a negative value, for example if it is a length.

WORKIT!

The rectangle shown below has length $(x + 8)$ cm and width $(x - 2)$ cm. The area of the rectangle is $56\,\text{cm}^2$. Find the value of x.

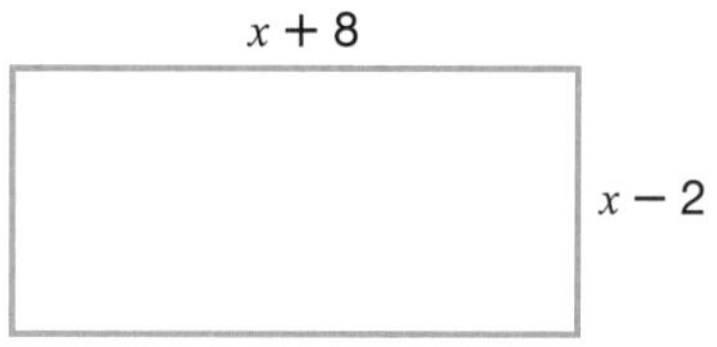

Area $= (x + 8)(x - 2) = x^2 + 6x - 16$

Also, area $= 56$ so $x^2 + 6x - 16 = 56$

Hence $x^2 + 6x - 72 = 0$

Factorising we obtain $(x - 6)(x + 12) = 0$ so $x = 6$ or -12

$x = -12$ would give a negative length and width so this is impossible.

So $x = 6\,\text{cm}$

DOIT!

Draw a poster showing the solution of a quadratic equation using factorisation, annotating the stages.

✓ CHECKIT!

1 Solve

  a $x^2 + 5x + 6 = 0$

  b $x^2 - x - 12 = 0$

  c $2x^2 + 17x + 35 = 0$

2 A right-angled triangle has base $(2x + 3)$ cm and height $(x + 4)$ cm. The area of the triangle is $9\,\text{cm}^2$.

  a Use the area of the triangle to show that $2x^2 - 11x - 6 = 0$.

  b Solve this equation to find the only possible value of x.

  c Work out the base and height of the triangle.

3 Three sides of a right-angled triangle are 13 cm, $(x + 1)$ cm and $(x + 8)$ cm. The longest side is the 13 cm side.

  Calculate the value of x.

Solving quadratic equations using the formula

NAILIT!

This formula will not be given so you will need to remember it.

Not all quadratic equations can be factorised easily. There are three other methods you can use: using a formula, completing the square or drawing a graph. Completing the square is covered on page 39 and finding solutions graphically on pages 40–2.

SNAPIT! Quadratic formula

Quadratic equations of the form $ax^2 + bx + c = 0$ can be solved using the formula:

$$x = \frac{-b \pm \sqrt{b^2 - 4ac}}{2a}$$

> Be careful with signs when you are entering numbers into this formula.

NAILIT!

Check your answers by substituting the values back into the equation.

WORKIT!

Solve the equation $2x^2 - 5x + 1 = 0$ leaving your answers in surd form.

$$x = \frac{-b \pm \sqrt{b^2 - 4ac}}{2a}$$

> Write down the formula.

$$x = \frac{-(-5) \pm \sqrt{(-5)^2 - 4(2)(1)}}{2(2)}$$

> Comparing the equation with $ax^2 + bx + c = 0$ gives $a = 2$, $b = -5$ and $c = 1$.
>
> Substitute these values into the formula.

$$= \frac{5 \pm \sqrt{25 - 8}}{4} = \frac{5 \pm \sqrt{17}}{4}$$

So $x = \dfrac{5 + \sqrt{17}}{4}$ or $\dfrac{5 - \sqrt{17}}{4}$

NAILIT!

If you are asked to leave your answer in surd form, then you must use either the formula or the method involving completing the square (see page 39).

WORKIT!

a Show that $\dfrac{3}{x + 7} = \dfrac{2 - x}{x + 1}$ can be written as $x^2 + 8x - 11 = 0$.

$$\frac{3}{x + 7} = \frac{2 - x}{x + 1}$$

> Multiply both sides by $(x + 1)(x + 7)$.

$$3(x + 1) = (2 - x)(x + 7)$$

$$3x + 3 = 2x + 14 - x^2 - 7x$$

> Expand the brackets.

$$3x + 3 = -x^2 - 5x + 14$$

$$x^2 + 8x - 11 = 0$$

> Rearrange in the form $ax^2 + bx + c = 0$.

b Hence solve the equation
$\frac{3}{x+7} = \frac{2-x}{x+1}$, giving your answers to 2 decimal places.

$$x = \frac{-b \pm \sqrt{b^2 - 4ac}}{2a}$$

$$= \frac{-8 \pm \sqrt{8^2 - 4(1)(-11)}}{2(1)}$$

 Substitute $a = 1$, $b = 8$ and $c = -11$ into the formula.

$$= \frac{-8 \pm \sqrt{64 + 44}}{2}$$

$$= \frac{-8 \pm \sqrt{108}}{2}$$

$$= \frac{-8 + \sqrt{108}}{2} \quad \text{or} \quad \frac{-8 - \sqrt{108}}{2}$$

$$= 1.1962 \quad \text{or} \quad -9.1962$$

$$= 1.20 \text{ or } -9.20 \text{ (to 2 d.p.)}$$

NAILIT!

If the question asks for the answer to be given to a certain number of decimal places, you need to use the formula rather than factorisation.

DOIT!

Use the quadratic formula to solve the equations you solved by factorisation in the previous section.

✓ CHECKIT!

1 Solve the equation $2x^2 - x - 7 = 0$, giving your answers correct to 3 significant figures.

2 a Show that $\frac{2x+3}{x+2} = 3x + 1$ can be written as $3x^2 + 5x - 1 = 0$.

b Hence solve the equation
$\frac{2x+3}{x+2} = 3x + 1$, giving your answers to 2 decimal places.

Solving simultaneous equations

Simultaneous equations are sets of equations that have more than one variable (e.g. x and y). Solving the equations means finding values for x and y that are true for both equations.

SNAPIT! Simultaneous equations

There are three methods that can be used to solve a pair of simultaneous equations:

1. **By elimination**: eliminate one of the unknowns by adding or subtracting the two simultaneous equations.

2. **By substitution**: substitute the expression for x or y from one of the equations into the other equation.

3. **Graphically**: use both equations to plot two lines – their point of intersection is the solution.

Solving simultaneous equations by elimination

Eliminate one of the variables by either adding or subtracting the equations.

WORKIT!

Solve the simultaneous equations.

$2x + 3y = 8$ (1)

$x + 4y = 9$ (2)

Number the equations so it is easier to refer to them.

$2x + 8y = 18$ (3)

Make the coefficients of either x or y the same for both equations, by multiplying one or both of the equations by numbers.

In this case, multiply equation (2) by 2 to make the coefficients of x the same.

Subtract (1) from (3).

$5y = 10$

$y = 2$

$2x + 3y = 8$ (1)

$2x + 3(2) = 8$ ← Substitute $y = 2$ into equation (1).

$2x + 6 = 8$

$2x = 2$

$x = 1$

$x + 4y = 9$ (2)

$1 + 4(2) = 9$ ← Check the answer by substituting $x = 1$ and $y = 2$ into equation (2).

Solution is $x = 1$ and $y = 2$.

NAILIT!

Always check your answer by substituting into the equations.

Solving simultaneous equations by substitution

This method of solving simultaneous equations involves removing y by substituting the y value from one of the equations into the other equation. The substitution method is preferred when finding the solutions to a ← non-linear equation and a linear equation.

> Non linear means it has a power of x, as in a quadratic equation.

WORKIT!

Solve the simultaneous equations.

$x^2 + y^2 = 16$ ←

> The first equation represents a circle because it is the form $x^2 + y^2 = r^2$. The second equation is a straight line because it is in the form $ax + by = c$.

$x + y = 4$

$x = 4 - y$ ←

> Rearrange the second equation to express x in terms of y.

$(4 - y)^2 + y^2 = 16$ ←

> Now substitute for x into the first equation.

$16 - 8y + y^2 + y^2 = 16$

$2y^2 - 8y = 0$ ←

> Subtract 16 from both sides.

$2y(y - 4) = 0$ ← Remove $2y$ as a factor.

$2y = 0$ giving $y = 0$, or $y - 4 = 0$ giving $y = 4$.

Substituting $y = 0$ into $x + y = 4$ gives $x = 4$. ←

> You can use either equation but this one is easier.

Substituting $y = 4$ into $x + y = 4$ gives $x = 0$.

So the solutions are $x = 4$ and $y = 0$, or $x = 0$ and $y = 4$.

NAILIT!

Make sure you write 'or' between the two sets of values, not 'and'.

Solving simultaneous equations graphically

Any pair of equations can be solved graphically by drawing them accurately and finding any point or points of intersection.

NAILIT!

When asked to plot a graph, create a table of values.

WORKIT!

Solve these simultaneous equations graphically, giving your solutions to 1 decimal place.

$y = x^2 - 4x + 1$

$y = x - 2$

x	0	1	2	3	4	5
$y = x^2 - 4x + 1$	1	-2	-3	-2	1	6

> This is a quadratic equation, so you need five or six pairs of coordinates to plot the graph.

x	0	2	5
$y = x - 2$	-2	0	3

> You only need two pairs of coordinates for a straight line, but a third one provides a check.

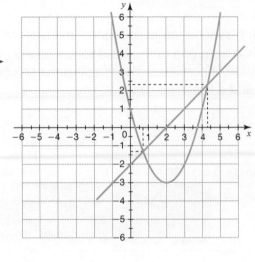

Plot the graphs of the two equations and find where they intersect.

NAIL IT!

Two linear equations could be solved in a similar way, but there would be only one point of intersection so only one pair of values.

The two pairs of solutions are:

$x = 4.3, y = 2.3$ and $x = 0.7, y = -1.3$

DO IT!

Create revision cards to show when each method of solving simultaneous equations is most appropriate.

STRETCH IT!

Not all simultaneous equations can be solved. If lines are parallel to each other there are no points of intersection.

✓ CHECK IT!

1 Solve these pairs of simultaneous equations.

   a $y = 3x - 7$
   $y = 3 - 2x$

   b $y = 2x - 6$
   $y = -3x + 14$

2 Solve the simultaneous equations.

   $y = 10x^2 - 5x - 2$
   $y = 2x - 3$

3 The line $y = 6x + 2$ and the curve $y = x^2 + 5x - 4$ intersect at two points. Use an algebraic method to find the coordinates of these points.

Solving inequalities

Representing inequalities

Number lines and set notation

Both number lines and set notation can be used to represent inequalities, as shown below.

> In set notation, { } contains the possible set of values.
>
> ∪ means that the set of numbers contains all the numbers represented by both inequalities.

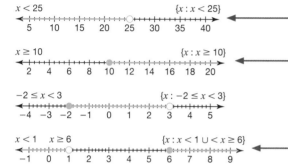

$x < 25$ $\{x : x < 25\}$

$x \geq 10$ $\{x : x \geq 10\}$

$-2 \leq x < 3$ $\{x : -2 \leq x < 3\}$

$x < 1$ $x \geq 6$ $\{x : x < 1 \cup < x \geq 6\}$

> The blue line shows x is less than 25. The open circle at 25 shows that x cannot be equal to 25.

> The blue line shows x is 10 or greater. The closed circle at 10 shows that x can be equal to 10.

> When there is a gap between the circles, two separate inequalities are represented.

Graphically

Inequalities can be shown graphically using boundary lines and shading. If the inequality allows points on the boundary line, then it is drawn as a solid line; otherwise it is a dotted line.

WORKIT!

Shade the region of points on a graph where

a $x \leq 3$

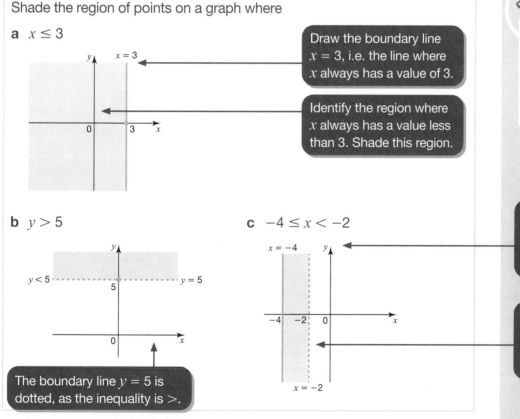

> Draw the boundary line $x = 3$, i.e. the line where x always has a value of 3.

> Identify the region where x always has a value less than 3. Shade this region.

b $y > 5$

c $-4 \leq x < -2$

> The boundary line $y = 5$ is dotted, as the inequality is $>$.

> Draw both boundary lines. Remember that $x = -4$ needs to be solid and $x = -2$ dotted.

> The shaded region is where x always has a value between -4 and -2.

NAILIT!

Always remember that the region that is allowed is the shaded region.

Linear inequalities

Solve inequalities in the same way as you solve equations, by doing the same operation to both sides of the inequality.

WORKIT!

Solve these inequalities.

a $4x - 5 > 2$

> Add 5 to both sides.

$$4x > 7$$

> Divide both sides by 4.

$$x > \frac{7}{4}$$

c $-3 \le 2x + 1 < 7$

$$-4 \le 2x < 6$$

> Subtract 1 from all three elements.

> Divide all three elements by 2.

$$-2 \le x < 3$$

b $3(2x - 7) \ge 12x + 15$

$$6x - 21 \ge 12x + 15$$

$$-6x - 21 \ge 15$$

$$-6x \ge 36$$

$$x \le -6$$

> When you multiply or divide by a negative number, reverse the inequality.

Linear inequalities with two variables

Sometimes you will be given two or three equations with two variables and asked to show the solution on a graph:

> To draw a straight line, substitute two values of x into the equation to find y, and draw the line through the two points.

1 Draw the lines representing boundary lines by replacing the inequality symbol with $=$. If the inequality is $\le$ or $\ge$ make the line solid; if it is $<$ or $>$ make the line dotted.

2 For each line, shade the region that is allowed.

> If you are not sure which side of the line to shade, substitute a pair of values for x and y.

NAIL IT!

If you can solve equations, you can solve inequalities. Don't be put off by the symbols!

NAIL IT!

Inequalities can be solved in a similar way to equations, but multiplying or dividing the inequality by a negative number means that the inequality sign must be **reversed**.

WORKIT!

a Illustrate the region represented by the following inequalities on a graph by shading the region that is required.

$$y \le x \qquad x + 3y \le 12 \qquad y > 1$$

b List the integer values of x and y that satisfy all of these inequalities.

> Draw the lines $y = x$, $x + 3y = 12$ as solid lines and $y = 1$ as a dotted line.

> Any point in the required region or on solid lines enclosing the region satisfies all three inequalities.

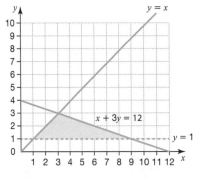

> To work out which side of $x + 3y = 12$ to shade, substitute $x = 1$ and $y = 4$: $1 + 3(4) = 13$. The inequality is $x + 3y \le 12$, so $(1, 4)$ is not allowed.

$(2, 2), (3, 2), (4, 2), (5, 2), (6, 2), (3, 3)$

Quadratic inequalities

To solve a quadratic inequality such as $x^2 + x \geq 6$:

1 Ensure that the quadratic inequality has all the terms on one side and a zero on the other side: $x^2 + x - 6 \geq 0$.

2 Consider the case where $x^2 + x - 6 = 0$.
Solve the equation:
$x^2 + x - 6 = (x + 3)(x - 2) = 0$, ◄——— These are the points where the curve cuts the x-axis.
so $x = -3$ or $x = 2$.

3 Sketch the curve $x^2 + x - 6$.

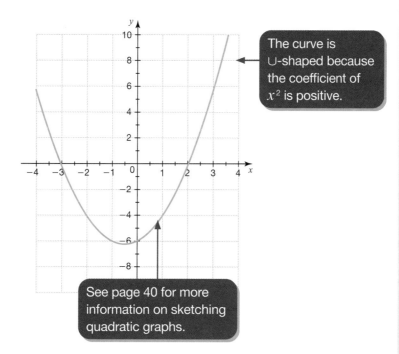

The curve is U-shaped because the coefficient of x^2 is positive.

See page 40 for more information on sketching quadratic graphs.

4 Identify the values of x where $x^2 + x - 6 \geq 0$.
These are the values of x for which y is greater than or equal to 0 – where the graph is above or on the x-axis: $x \leq -3$ and $x \geq 2$.

For the opposite inequality ($x^2 + x - 6 \leq 0$), the values of x would be for the graph on or below the x-axis: $-3 \leq x \leq 2$.

WORKIT!

a Solve the inequality $x^2 - 7x + 10 < 0$.

$x^2 - 7x + 10 = 0$ gives $(x - 2)(x - 5) = 0$, so the curve intersects the x-axis at $x = 2$ and $x = 5$.

> Work out the solutions to $x^2 - 7x + 10 = 0$ and sketch the curve, marking the roots of the quadratic.

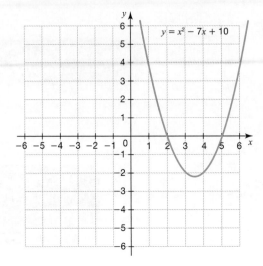

$y = x^2 - 7x + 10$

Solution is $2 < x < 5$.

> Identify the values of x for the graph below the x-axis because of the $<$ in the inequality.

b Show the solutions on a number line.

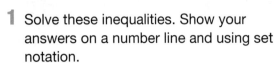

DOIT!

Make up some inequalities, rolling dice to generate the numbers. Solve them.

✓ CHECKIT!

1 Solve these inequalities. Show your answers on a number line and using set notation.

a $1 - 2x < -11$ **c** $\dfrac{x - 5}{3} < 7$

b $2x - 7 \geq 15$

2 Solve these inequalities.

a $2x - 4 > x + 6$

b $4 + x < 6 - 4x$

c $2x + 9 \geq 5(x - 3)$

3 a Illustrate the region represented by the following inequalities on a graph.

$x > -1$ $y \leq 2$ $x - y < 2$

b List the integer values of x and y that satisfy all of these inequalities.

4 Solve the inequality $x^2 > 3x + 10$.

Problem solving using algebra

Problems involving simultaneous equations

In some questions you will have to form the two simultaneous equations from information given in the question and then solve them.

WORKIT!

The sum of two numbers is 14 and the difference of the same numbers is 2. Find the two numbers.

Let the larger number $= x$ and the smaller number $= y$.

$$x + y = 14 \qquad (1)$$

$$x - y = 2 \qquad (2)$$

Create the simultaneous equations from the information in the question.

Add equations (1) and (2).

$$2x = 16$$

$$x = 8$$

Substitute $x = 8$ into equation (1).

$$x + y = 14$$

$$8 + y = 14$$

$$y = 6$$

Check:

$$x - y = 2 \qquad (2)$$

Substitute $x = 8$ and $y = 6$ into equation (2).

$$8 - 6 = 2$$

$$2 = 2$$

Both sides of the equation are equal, showing that the values of x and y satisfy equation (2).

The two numbers are 6 and 8.

Problems involving inequalities

In some problems, you will be given a maximum or minimum value (e.g. length, area, volume). You then set up an inequality and solve it.

WORKIT!

This solid cuboid has length $4x$ cm, width $2x$ cm and height x cm, where x is an integer.

The total surface area of the cuboid is less than or equal to 2800 cm^2.

Show that $x \leq 10$.

Area of top + bottom = $8x^2 + 8x^2 = 16x^2$

Area of front + back = $4x^2 + 4x^2 = 8x^2$

Area of the two sides = $2x^2 + 2x^2 = 4x^2$

Total surface area = $16x^2 + 8x^2 + 4x^2 = 28x^2$

> Find an expression for the total surface area in terms of x.

$28x^2 \leq 2800$

> Express the total surface area as an inequality.

$x^2 \leq 100$

$x \leq 10$

> $\sqrt{100} = \pm 10$, but it would not make sense for x to be negative when finding the sides of the cuboid.

DOIT!

Design a poster to show how to turn a word problem into an algebraic expression.

CHECKIT!

1 Find two numbers such that their sum is 77 and their difference is 25.

2 A number is added to the numerator and denominator of the fraction $\frac{15}{31}$.

The resulting fraction is $\frac{5}{6}$. Find the number.

3 The perimeter of a rectangle is 24 cm and its area is 27 cm^2.

Find the length and width of the rectangle.

Use of functions

A **function** takes a number as **input** and gives another number as **output**.

The function is represented as a box and it does something mathematical to the number you input. Whatever the input it performs the same mathematical operation or operations on it to give the output.

This function can be written as
$f(x) = \frac{x}{3} + 1$.

When applied to the number 18,
it is expressed as $f(18) = \frac{18}{3} + 1 = 7$.

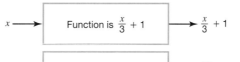

Similarly, the function 'square x and then add x' can be written as $f(x) = x^2 + x$.

When applied to the number 3, it is expressed as $f(3) = 3^2 + 3 = 12$. ⟵ Replace x with 3.

WORKIT!

$f(x) = x^2 - 2x + 1$

Work out

a $f(2)$ ⟵ Substitute $x = 2$ in $x^2 - 2x + 1$.

$f(2) = 2^2 - 2(2) + 1 = 1$

b $f(-1)$

$f(-1) = (-1)^2 - 2(-1) + 1 = 4$ ⟵ Put brackets around negative numbers.

c the values of x for which $f(x) = 0$.

When $f(x) = 0$, $x^2 - 2x + 1 = 0$ ⟵ This is a quadratic equation that needs to be factorised and then solved.

$(x - 1)(x - 1) = 0$

So $x = 1$

Inverse functions

The **inverse** of a function will produce the input value from the output value. The inverse of the function $f(x)$ is written as $f^{-1}(x)$.

SNAPIT! Inverse functions

To find the inverse of a function:

1 Let the function equal y.

2 Rearrange the resulting equation so that x is the subject of the equation.

3 Replace x with $f^{-1}(x)$ and replace y with x.

WORKIT!

$f(x) = \frac{x}{3} + 1$. Find $f^{-1}(x)$.

Let $y = \frac{x}{3} + 1$

$3y = x + 3$

> Rearrange to make x the subject. First multiply both sides by 3 to remove the denominator.

$x = 3y - 3$

$f^{-1}(x) = 3x - 3$

> Replace x with $f^{-1}(x)$ and replace y with x.

Composite functions

Composite functions involve applying two or more functions in succession.

Consider the following example:

$f(x) = x^2$ and $g(x) = x - 2$

The composite function $fg(x)$ means $f(g(x))$ and is the result of performing the function g first and then the function f.

> Here, g means 'subtract 2 from it' and f means 'square it'. So fg means 'subtract 2 from it' and then 'square it', i.e. $(x - 2)^2$. gf means 'square it' and then 'subtract 2 from it', i.e. $x^2 - 2$.

To find $fg(x)$, replace x by the expression for $g(x)$ in $f(x)$:

$fg(x) = f(g(x)) = f(x - 2) = (x - 2)^2$

WORKIT!

The functions f and g are such that $f(x) = 3(x + 1)$ and $g(x) = \frac{x}{3} + 2$.

Find

a g(12)

$g(12) = \frac{12}{3} + 2 = 4 + 2 = 6$

b $g^{-1}(x)$

Let $y = \frac{x}{3} + 2$

$3y = x + 6$

$x = 3y - 6$

$g^{-1}(x) = 3x - 6$

c fg(x)

$fg(x) = 3\left(\left(\frac{x}{3} + 2\right) + 1\right)$

$= 3\left(\frac{x}{3} + 3\right)$

$= x + 9$

DOIT!

Find an inverse function using both the function machine method and the algebraic method.

✓ CHECKIT!

1 $f(x) = \frac{1}{x - 1}$ where $x \neq 1$.

Find

a f(0)   **b** $f\left(-\frac{1}{2}\right)$ **c** $f^{-1}(x)$

2 $f(x) = \sqrt{(x^2 - 9)}$ and $g(x) = x + 4$.

Find

a fg(x)   **b** gf(x)   **c** gf(3)

Iterative methods

Iteration means repeatedly performing a function, each time using your previous answer to get the next result. Iterative methods enable equations to be solved that would be hard to solve using other methods.

Using changes of sign of f(x) to locate solutions

If f(x) can take any value between a and b, and there is a change of sign between f(a) and f(b), then a solution of f(x) = 0 lies between a and b.

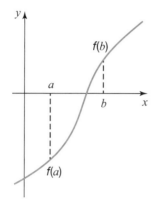

WORKIT!

Show that the equation

$9x^3 - 9x + 1 = 0$

has a solution between 0 and 0.2. ◄ a and b are 0 and 0.2, respectively.

Let $f(x) = 9x^3 - 9x + 1$

$f(0) = 1$

$f(0.2) = 9(0.2)^3 - 9(0.2) + 1 = 0.072 - 1.8 + 1 = -0.728$

Insert each value for x into the function and see if there is a sign change between f(0) and f(0.2).

As there is a sign change, there is a solution between 0 and 0.2.

Entering values into a recurrence relation to solve an equation

A recurrence relation gives a value in terms of the previous value. Recurrence relations can be used to solve equations, i.e. find a **root**. ◄

A root of an equation is a value of x where the function equals 0, i.e. where its graph crosses the x-axis.

WORKIT!

The subscript tags n and $n + 1$ mean that there is a series of values for x, and each solution is used to generate the next one, using this function. We start with $n = 0$.

The recurrence relation

$$x_{n+1} = \left(\frac{2x_n + 5}{4}\right)^{\frac{1}{3}}$$

with $x_0 = 1.2$, may be used to find a, a root of the equation $4x^3 - 2x - 5 = 0$.

a is one of the roots of the equations (i.e. a solution).

Find and record the values of x_1, x_2, x_3 and x_4.

Write down the value of x_4 correct to 5 decimal places and prove that this value is the value of the root a correct to 5 decimal places.

To get x_1, substitute the value for x_0 into the equation. Then substitute x_1 to find x_2, and so on.

$x_0 = 1.2$

$x_1 = \left(\frac{2x_0 + 5}{4}\right)^{\frac{1}{3}} = \left(\frac{2(1.2) + 5}{4}\right)^{\frac{1}{3}} = 1.227601026$

$x_2 = \left(\frac{2x_1 + 5}{4}\right)^{\frac{1}{3}} = \left(\frac{2(1.227601026) + 5}{4}\right)^{\frac{1}{3}} = 1.230645994$

$x_3 = \left(\frac{2x_2 + 5}{4}\right)^{\frac{1}{3}} = \left(\frac{2(1.230645994) + 5}{4}\right)^{\frac{1}{3}} = 1.230980996$

$x_4 = \left(\frac{2x_3 + 5}{4}\right)^{\frac{1}{3}} = \left(\frac{2(1.230980996) + 5}{4}\right)^{\frac{1}{3}}$

Do not round these numbers yet.

$= 1.231017841$

Round the final answer to the required number of decimal places.

$x_4 = 1.23102$ (to 5 d.p.)

The root lies on the x-axis where f(x) = 0. Test x values either side of your answer by putting them into the function. If one output is positive and one negative, your answer is in the right range and is correct.

DOIT!

Draw a flowchart for using iteration to find a root to a specified accuracy.

f(1.231015) = 4(1.231015)³ − 2(1.231015) − 5 = −0.000119668

f(1.231025) = 4(1.231025)³ − 2(1.231025) − 5 = 0.000042182

As there is a sign change between these values of f(x), 1.23102 is in the correct range.

✓ CHECKIT!

1 The cubic equation $x^3 - x - 2 = 0$ has a root a between 1 and 2.

The recurrence relation

$$x_{n+1} = (x_n + 2)^{\frac{1}{3}}$$

with $x_0 = 1.5$ can be used to find a.

Calculate x_4, giving your answer correct to 3 decimal places. Prove that this value is also the value of a correct to 3 decimal places.

Equation of a straight line

Straight-line graphs are also called **linear** graphs and have an equation of the form:

$y = mx + c$ ← There is a single y on the left-hand side of the equation.

m is the **gradient** (i.e. the steepness of the line) and c is the **intercept on the y-axis** (where the graph cuts the y-axis).

It is important that in this equation there is only an x term. There are no terms containing x^2, x^3, $\sqrt{x}$, $\frac{1}{x}$, and so on.

This is an equation of a straight line: $y = 2x - 3$.

Comparing this equation with $y = mx + c$, the gradient, m, is 2 and the intercept on the y-axis, c, is -3.

NAILIT!

For an equation to be that of a straight line, you must be able to rearrange it in the form $y = mx + c$ (with no higher power than x).

WORKIT!

Which of these equations are straight lines? Explain your answer.

a $y = 1.4x + 7$

Yes: in the form $y = mx + c$.

b $y = 4x^2 + 1$

No: not in the form $y = mx + c$ as it contains a term in x^2.

c $y = \frac{2}{x}$

No: not in the form $y = mx + c$.

d $5x + 2y = 3$

Yes: can be rearranged to give $2y = -5x + 3$ and this can be divided by 2 to give $y = -\frac{5}{2}x + \frac{3}{2}$, which is in the form $y = mx + c$.

Gradients of straight-line graphs

Gradients have a sign and a value, for example -0.6 and 4. ← The gradient of a line is the steepness of the line.

The sign of the gradient

The gradient of a straight line can be positive (if y increases as x increases), negative (if y decreases as x increases) or zero (if the value of y stays the same as x increases).

SNAPIT! Straight-line graphs

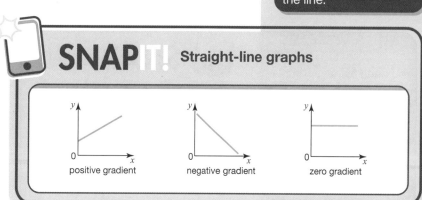

positive gradient   negative gradient   zero gradient

Finding the gradient

To find the size of the gradient, draw a triangle as shown. Then use this relationship for the gradient:

Gradient, $m = \dfrac{\text{change in } y \text{ values}}{\text{change in } x \text{ values}}$

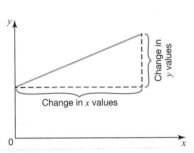

To determine whether the gradient is positive or negative, look at which way the line slopes. Only include the sign if the gradient is negative. If the gradient is positive, say 4, do not write +4.

Finding the gradient of a straight line joining two points

SNAP IT!   Gradient of a line

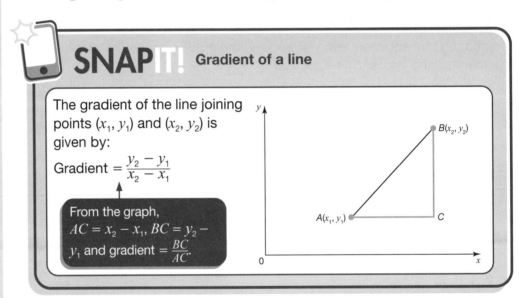

The gradient of the line joining points (x_1, y_1) and (x_2, y_2) is given by:

Gradient $= \dfrac{y_2 - y_1}{x_2 - x_1}$

From the graph, $AC = x_2 - x_1$, $BC = y_2 - y_1$ and gradient $= \dfrac{BC}{AC}$.

WORKIT!

Find the gradient of the straight line joining the points A(−3, 2) and B(1, 6).

$\text{Gradient} = \dfrac{6 - 2}{1 - (-3)} = \dfrac{4}{4} = 1$

Take care with the signs. Make sure that you give the x and y coordinates in the same order.

Finding the midpoint of a straight line

NAILIT!

You need to remember this formula as it will not be given in the formula booklet.

SNAP IT!

Midpoint of a line

The midpoint of the line joining the points (x_1, y_1) and (x_2, y_2) is given by:

$\left(\dfrac{x_1 + x_2}{2}, \dfrac{y_1 + y_2}{2}\right)$

WORKIT!

Find the midpoint of the line joining the two points with coordinates (2, 6) and (8, 4).

$\left(\dfrac{2 + 8}{2}, \dfrac{6 + 4}{2}\right) = (5, 5)$

Finding the equation of a straight line

Given the gradient and y-intercept

Given the gradient of a line, m, and the intercept on the y-axis, c, you can write down the equation of the line.

WORKIT!

Find the equation of the line shown.

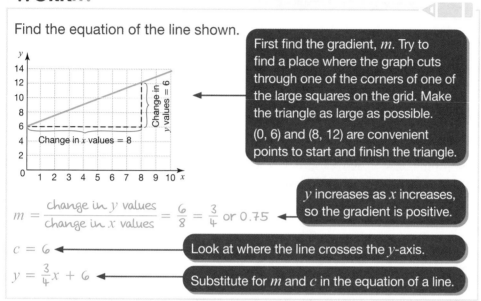

First find the gradient, m. Try to find a place where the graph cuts through one of the corners of one of the large squares on the grid. Make the triangle as large as possible.

(0, 6) and (8, 12) are convenient points to start and finish the triangle.

y increases as x increases, so the gradient is positive.

$$m = \frac{\text{change in } y \text{ values}}{\text{change in } x \text{ values}} = \frac{6}{8} = \frac{3}{4} \text{ or } 0.75$$

$c = 6$ ← Look at where the line crosses the y-axis.

$y = \frac{3}{4}x + 6$ ← Substitute for m and c in the equation of a line.

Given the gradient and the coordinates of a point

SNAPIT! Equation of a straight line

The equation of a straight line with gradient m and which passes through a point (x_1, y_1) is given by:

$$y - y_1 = m(x - x_1)$$

NAILIT!

You need to remember the formula for the equation of a straight line as it will not be given in the formula booklet.

WORKIT!

Find the equation of the straight line with a gradient of 2 that passes through the point (2, 5).

$y - 5 = 2(x - 2)$ ← Substitute for m, x_1 and y_1.

$y - 5 = 2x - 4$ ← Expand the brackets and rearrange into the form $y = mx + c$.

$y = 2x + 1$

This is in the form $y = mx + c$, so you can immediately see that $m = 2$ and c (the intercept on the y-axis) is 1.

Parallel and perpendicular lines

Parallel lines

For two lines to be **parallel** to each other, they must have the same gradient.

For example, the equation of the line that is parallel to the line $y = 3x - 2$ and intersects the y-axis at $y = 4$ is:

$y = 3x + 4$ ◄─── $m = 3$ and $c = 4$

Perpendicular lines

When two lines are **perpendicular** to each other (i.e. they make an angle of 90°), the product (multiple) of their gradients is -1.

If one line has a gradient m_1 and the other a gradient of m_2 then:

$m_1 m_2 = -1$

For example, if a straight line has gradient $-\frac{1}{3}$, then the gradient of the line perpendicular to this is given by:

$\left(-\frac{1}{3}\right) m_2 = -1$ so gradient $m_2 = 3$.

NAIL IT!

You may be asked to find the equation of a straight line through two points. First find the gradient. Then substitute m and one pair of coordinates into $y = mx + c$.

DO IT!

Write a revision card for the different ways of finding the equation of a straight line.

Reciprocal means 'one over' a value, or that value to the power -1.

NAIL IT!

A quick way to find the gradient of a line that is perpendicular is to write the reciprocal of the gradient of the original line and change the sign $\left(\text{i.e. } -\frac{1}{\text{original gradient}}\right)$.

✓ CHECK IT!

1 A straight line has the equation $2y = 4x - 5$.

  a Write down the gradient of the line.

  A line is drawn perpendicular to this line.

  b Write down the gradient of the perpendicular line.

  The perpendicular line crosses the y-axis at (0, 5).

  c Write down the equation of the line.

2 Find the equation of the line that has gradient 3 and passes through the point (2, 3).

3 A line has a gradient of 2 and passes through the point $(-1, 0)$.

  Find the equation of the line in the form $ay + bx + c = 0$.

4 A straight line passes through the points $A(-2, 0)$ and $B(6, 4)$.

  a Find the gradient of the line AB.

  b The midpoint of AB is M. Find the coordinates of M.

  c A straight line is drawn through point M which is perpendicular to the line AB.

    i Write down the gradient of this line.

    ii Find the equation of this line.

Quadratic graphs

Completing the square

Completing the square can be used to:

- solve quadratic equations
- help draw a quadratic graph by finding turning points.

Completing the square: coefficient of $x^2 = 1$

To complete the square for the quadratic $x^2 - 2x + 7$:

① Separate the x terms from the constant: $(x^2 - 2x) + 7$.

② Write the perfect square to give the x^2 and x terms: $(x - 1)^2$.

③ Then subtract a constant to make the identity true: $x^2 - 2x \equiv (x - 1)^2 - 1$.

④ Combine this with the constant in the original quadratic:

$$x^2 - 2x + 7 = (x - 1)^2 - 1 + 7$$
$$= (x - 1)^2 + 6$$

> The **coefficient** of x^2 is the number in front of x^2. If the first term is just x^2, the coefficient is 1.

> This example only used integers, but the method also works with fractions.

Completing the square: coefficient of $x^2 = 2$

To complete the square for the quadratic $2x^2 - 6x + 5$:

① Remove the coefficient of x^2 to outside a bracket: $2\left[x^2 - 3x + \frac{5}{2}\right]$.

② Use the method above to complete the square for the contents of the square bracket: $2\left[\left(x - \frac{3}{2}\right)^2 - \frac{9}{4} + \frac{5}{2}\right] = 2\left[\left(x - \frac{3}{2}\right)^2 + \frac{1}{4}\right]$.

③ Multiply the expression found by the number outside: $2\left(x - \frac{3}{2}\right)^2 + \frac{1}{2}$

So, $2x^2 - 6x + 5 = 2\left(x - \frac{3}{2}\right)^2 + \frac{1}{2}$.

Solving a quadratic equation by completing the square

Quadratic equations can be solved by completing the square.

WORKIT!

a Show that $x^2 + 6x + 4$ may be expressed in the form $(x + 3)^2 - 5$.

$$x^2 + 6x + 4 = (x + 3)^2 - 9 + 4$$
$$= (x + 3)^2 - 5$$

b Use your answer to part a to solve the quadratic equation $x^2 + 6x + 4 = 0$, giving your answers to 2 decimal places.

$$x^2 + 6x + 4 = 0$$
$$(x + 3)^2 - 5 = 0$$
$$(x + 3)^2 = 5$$
$$x + 3 = \pm\sqrt{5}$$
$$x = -3 + \sqrt{5} \text{ or } x = -3 - \sqrt{5}$$
$$x = -0.76 \text{ or } x = -5.24 \text{ (to 2 d.p.)}$$

> You must include both the positive and negative values when you square-root a number, giving two roots (i.e. solutions) rather than just one.

NAILIT!

You must use completing the square to solve the quadratic equation. You will lose marks if a method is specified in the question and you use a different method.

Sketching a quadratic graph

The shape of the graph of the quadratic equation $y = ax^2 + bx + c$ depends on the sign of a. The curve is ∪-shaped if a is positive and ∩-shaped if a is negative.

Finding the point or points where the curve intersects the x-axis

It is important to note that not all quadratic graphs intersect the x-axis.

'Intersect' means 'to cross'.

To find where the graph intersects the x-axis, solve the equation $ax^2 + bx + c = 0$. These values of x are called the **roots** of the equation. Mark the root(s) of x on the x-axis.

NAILIT!

Check the question to see if you should give your answer to a certain number of significant figures or decimal places.

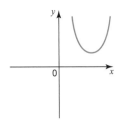

This graph does not intersect the x-axis so there are no roots

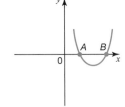

This graph intersects the x-axis in two places so there are two roots.

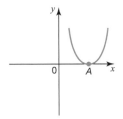

This graph intersects the x-axis in only one place so there is one root.

Finding turning points by completing the square

The **turning points** on a curve are the points where the gradient of the curve is zero. For a quadratic graph this will be a **maximum** point if the curve is ∩-shaped or a **minimum** point if the curve is ∪-shaped.

When the square has been completed, the equation for the curve will look like:

$y = a(x + p)^2 + q$

When $x = -p$, the value of the bracket is zero and, since the bracket is squared, this is its minimum value (since it cannot be negative). So the minimum value of y is q.

The turning point will be at $(-p, q)$.

The axis of symmetry will be the line $x = -p$.

For example, for $y = 2(x + 2)^2 - 1$, $a = 2$, $p = 2$ and $q = -1$.

The curve will be ∪-shaped with a minimum point at $(-2, -1)$ and an axis of symmetry of $x = -2$.

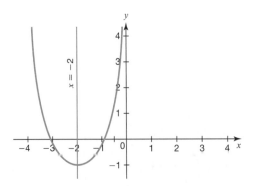

The maximum and minimum points of curves are called turning points as the gradient changes sign either side of the point. In this curve the gradient to the left is negative and to the right is positive. The gradient at the turning point itself is zero.

WORKIT!

a Express $4x^2 - 12x + 9$ in the form $a(x + b)^2 + c$.
Give the values of a, b and c.

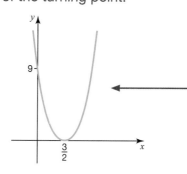

$4x^2 - 12x + 9 = 4\left[x^2 - 3x + \frac{9}{4}\right]$

> Write the coefficient of x^2 as a factor of the expression.

$= 4\left[\left(x - \frac{3}{2}\right)^2 - \frac{9}{4} + \frac{9}{4}\right]$

$= 4\left(x - \frac{3}{2}\right)^2$

$a = 4, b = -\frac{3}{2}, c = 0$

> Compare the expression with $a(x + b)^2 + c$.

b Hence sketch the graph of $y = 4x^2 - 12x + 9$, including the coordinates of the turning point.

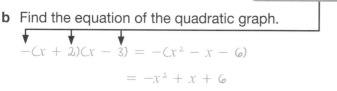

> The coefficient of x^2 is positive, so the graph is $\cup$-shaped.

> At the minimum point, $x = \frac{3}{2}$. When $x = \frac{3}{2}, y = 0$
> The coordinates of the turning point are $\left(\frac{3}{2}, 0\right)$.

WORKIT!

This is a quadratic graph.

> The graph is $\cap$-shaped, so the coefficient of x^2 is negative. Use the roots to write the factors of the quadratic.

a Write down the roots of the graph.

$x = -2$ and $x = 3$

b Find the equation of the quadratic graph.

$-(x + 2)(x - 3) = -(x^2 - x - 6)$

$= -x^2 + x + 6$

The equation is $y = -x^2 + x + 6$.

c Use the graph to estimate the solutions to $-x^2 + x + 6 = 2$.

$x = -1.55$ and $x = 2.55$

> Estimate the x values when $y = 2$.

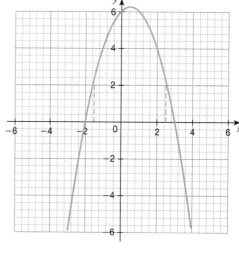

DOIT!

Produce a poster showing the information you need to sketch a quadratic graph.

CHECKIT!

1 **a** Write $2x^2 - 12x + 1$ in the form $a(x + b)^2 + c$, where a, b and c are integers.

b Hence or otherwise, for the graph $y = 2x^2 - 12x + 1$

   i find the coordinates of the turning point

   ii find the roots to 1 decimal place.

c Sketch the graph of $y = 2x^2 - 12x + 1$.

2 Write the equation for each quadratic graph.

a

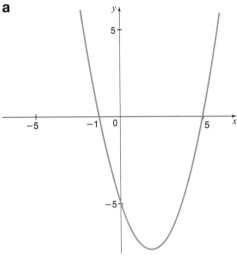

b

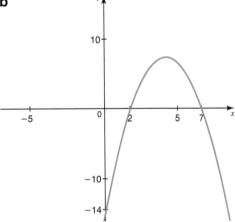

3 **a** Write $x^2 + 12x - 16$ in the form $(x + a)^2 + b$.

b Write down the coordinates of the turning point of the graph of $y = x^2 + 12x - 16$.

Recognising and sketching graphs of functions

Drawing cubic graphs

Cubic graphs have an x^3 term and have an equation of the form:

$y = ax^3 + bx^2 + cx + d$

where a, b, c and d are constants and where b, c or d could be zero.

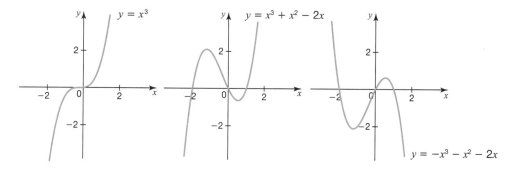

Graph has one root and no turning points.

Graph has two turning points and three roots.

Graph has two turning points and three roots.

WORKIT!

Draw the graph of $y = x^3 + x^2 - 6x$ between $x = -4$ and $x = 3$.

When $x = -4$, $y = (-4)^3 + (-4)^2 - 6(-4) = -24$.

x	−4	−3	−2	−1	0	1	2	3
$y = x^3 + x^2 - 6x$	−24	0	8	6	0	−4	0	18

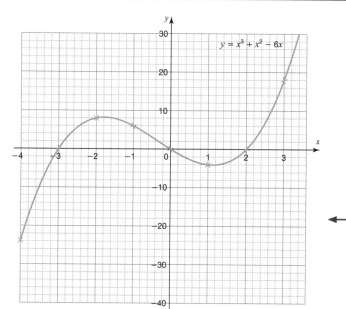

Draw a table and substitute each value of x into the equation to find the value of y. (The first substitution is shown here.)

NAILIT!

When substituting into an expression with many terms, it is best to write the calculation down.

Plot the points in the table and join them with a smooth curve.

NAILIT!

When plotting a graph:

- make sure you label the axes
- include the equation of the line/curve
- make sure the origin is marked
- do not draw the graph past the x coordinates that were specified
- join the points with a smooth curve.

NAILIT!

Often the questions on sketching graphs will give a series of graphs and a series of equations for you to match each equation to the correct graph.

Exponential functions are ones in the form $y = a^x$. You will only see exponential functions where a is a positive number.

Recognising sketch graphs

You looked at sketching quadratic graphs in the previous section. You also need to be able to recognise and sketch graphs of the following functions.

Reciprocal function   **Cubic function**   **Exponential function**

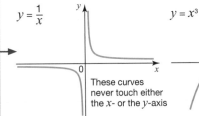

$y = \dfrac{1}{x}$

These curves never touch either the x- or the y-axis

$y = x^3$

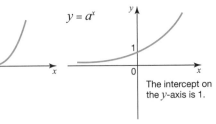

$y = a^x$

The intercept on the y-axis is 1.

The trigonometric functions

You need to know about the three trigonometric functions, **sine**, **cosine** and **tangent** – often abbreviated to sin, cos and tan.

The sine graph, $y = \sin x$

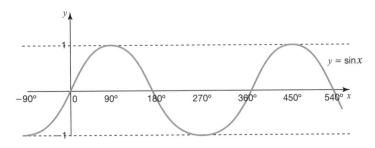

The cosine graph, $y = \cos x$

NAILIT!

If you are asked to draw a sketch graph, make sure you label the x- and y-axes and the origin and write the equation next to the curve. You may also be asked to mark the coordinates of any points where the curve crosses the axes.

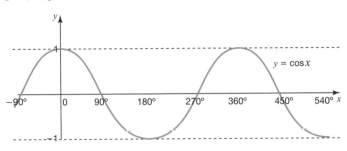

The tangent graph, $y = \tan x$

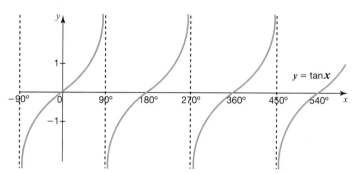

Using the trigonometric graphs to find angles

These graphs can be used to find angles.

WORKIT!

1 Find all the values of the angle θ in the range $0° \leq \theta \leq 360°$ satisfying $2\sin\theta = 1$.

$2\sin\theta = 1$

$\sin\theta = \frac{1}{2}$

$\theta = \sin^{-1}\left(\frac{1}{2}\right)$ ← Sin^{-1} means 'angle with a sine of'.

$\theta = 30°$

Also, $\theta = 180 - 30 = 150°$ ← The line $y = 0.5$ (or $y = \frac{1}{2}$) lets you read off the values for the angle.

Hence $\theta = 30°, 150°$

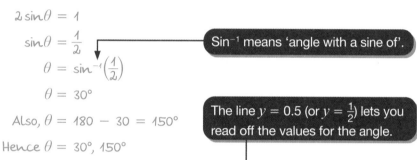

2 The graph shows the curve $y = \sin x$ in the interval $0° \leq x \leq 720°$.

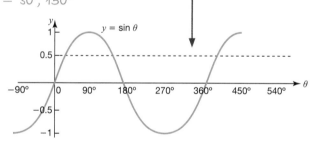

a Write down the coordinates of all the points of intersection with the x-axis.

$(0, 0), (180, 0), (360, 0), (540, 0), (720, 0)$

b Write down the coordinates of all the turning points for this graph.

$(90, 1), (270, -1), (450, 1), (630, -1)$

DOIT!

Type an equation into an internet search engine and find out what the graph looks like.

Make a small change to the equation and search again to see how this changes the graph.

To produce the graph $y = x^3$, you need to enter the equation as $y = x\,^{\wedge}3$ as the $^{\wedge}$ symbol is used to indicate a power or **exponential**.

CHECKIT!

1 Here are the equations of six graphs.

a $y = 5x^3$

b $y = \cos x$

c $y = 3^x$

d $y = x^2 - 4x + 4$

e $y = \sin x$

f $y = \dfrac{2}{x}$

Match each equation to one of the graphs A to F.

A
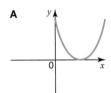

B
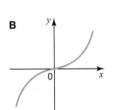

C
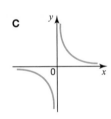

D
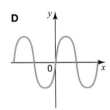

E
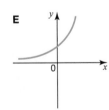

F
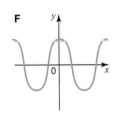

2 a Sketch the graph of $y = \tan x$ for $0° \le x \le 360°$.

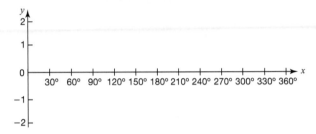

b One solution to $\tan x = \sqrt{3}$ is $x = 60°$.

Find another solution for x in the range $0° \le x \le 360°$.

3 Here are the equations of four graphs. Match each equation to one of the graphs A to G.

a $y = 1 - x$

b $y = 2x - 1$

c $y = x^2 - 3$

d $y = 3 - x^2$

A
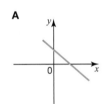

B
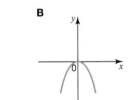

C
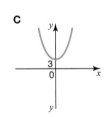

D
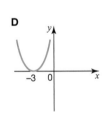

E
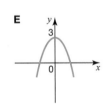

F
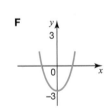

G
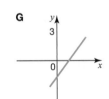

Translations and reflections of functions

Translating the graph of $y = f(x)$

A **translation** is a vertical movement, a horizontal movement or both. If you are given a graph of a function in the form $y = f(x)$, then the graph of a new function may be obtained from the original graph by applying a translation.

$y = f(x)$ translated to $y = f(x + a)$ is a **translation** of $-a$ units **parallel to the x-axis**. The whole curve moves a units to the left. Similarly, $y = f(x - b)$ is a translation of b units to the right.

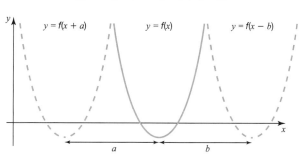

$y = f(x)$ translated to $y = f(x) + a$ is a **translation** of a units **parallel to the y-axis**. If a is positive, the whole graph moves up a units and if a is negative it moves down by a units.

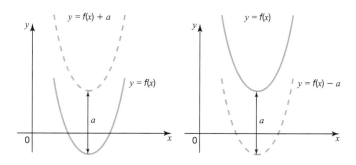

Reflecting the graph of $y = f(x)$

$y = -f(x)$ is a **reflection** of $y = f(x)$ **in the x-axis**.

$y = f(-x)$ is a **reflection** of $y = f(x)$ **in the y-axis**.

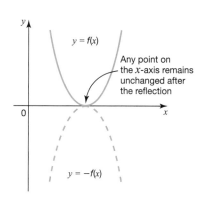

Any point on the x-axis remains unchanged after the reflection

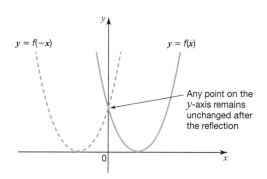

Any point on the y-axis remains unchanged after the reflection

WORKIT!

1 The diagram shows a sketch of the graph $y = f(x)$. The graph passes through the points (1, 0) and (5, 0) and has a turning point at (3, −4).

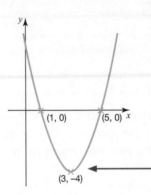

> A turning point is a point on the curve where the gradient is zero. This will occur at any maximum or minimum points.

Sketch the following graphs, using a separate set of axes for each graph. In each case, indicate the coordinates of the turning point and the coordinates of the points of intersection of the graph with the x-axis.

a $y = f(x + 1)$

b $y = -f(x)$

> $y = f(x + 1)$ is a translation of $y = f(x)$ by one unit to the left parallel to the x-axis).

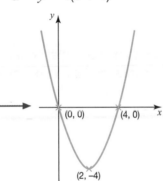

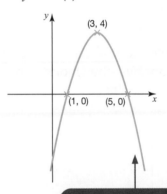

> The negative sign is before f(x), so this is a reflection in the x-axis.

Combinations of reflections and translations

Translations and reflections can be combined. The order in which they are carried out does not matter.

Here are some combinations of reflections and translations for this graph of $y = f(x)$.

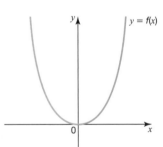

NAILIT!

Remember to add the coordinates of the points of intersection with the x-axis and of the turning point. You would lose marks if you only put the x coordinates of these points on the x-axis.

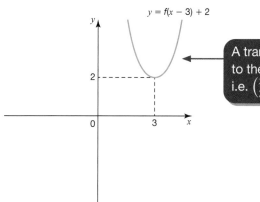

A translation of 3 units to the right and 2 up i.e. $\binom{3}{2}$

DO IT!

Draw a poster summarising translations and transformations of functions.

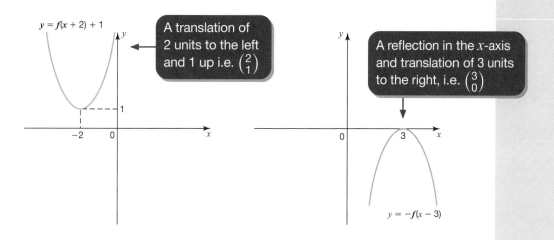

A translation of 2 units to the left and 1 up i.e. $\binom{2}{1}$

A reflection in the x-axis and translation of 3 units to the right, i.e. $\binom{3}{0}$

CHECK IT!

1 The diagram shows the graph of $y = f(x)$. The graph has a turning point at (2, 5) and intersects the x-axis at the points (−2, 0) and (6, 0).

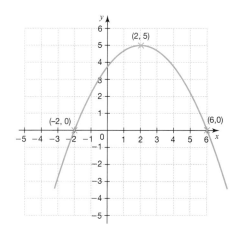

Write down the coordinates of the turning point of the curve with equation

a $y = f(x − 1)$ **c** $y = −f(x)$

b $y = f(x + 3)$ **d** $y = f(−x)$

2 The diagram shows the graph of $y = f(x)$. The graph has a maximum point at (1, 2).

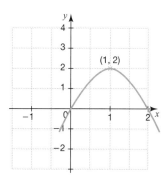

Sketch the following graphs, using a separate set of axes for each graph. Mark the coordinates of the turning point on each graph.

a $y = f(x − 1)$ **c** $y = −f(x − 1)$

b $y = f(x) + 2$ **d** $y = f(x − 1) + 2$

Equation of a circle and tangent to a circle

Equation of a circle

SNAPIT!   Equation of a circle

The equation of a circle with centre the origin (0, 0) and radius r is:
$$x^2 + y^2 = r^2$$

So the equation $x^2 + y^2 = 25$ represents the equation of circle with centre at the origin and with a radius of 5.

WORKIT!

A circle has the equation $x^2 + y^2 = 9$.

a Write down the coordinates of the centre of the circle and give the radius of the circle.

Centre is at (0, 0).

Radius = 3

> Comparing with $x^2 + y^2 = r^2$, $r^2 = 9$.

b Prove that the point P $(\sqrt{3}, \sqrt{6})$ lies on the circle.

If these points lie on the circle, then:

$x^2 + y^2 = (\sqrt{3})^2 + (\sqrt{6})^2$

$= 9$

> If the point lies on the circle its coordinates will satisfy the equation of the circle.

This is the same as the right-hand side of the equation of the circle. The point therefore satisfies the equation and so lies on the circle.

Equation of a tangent to a circle

The tangent to a circle is perpendicular to the radius. Using the coordinates of where the tangent touches the circle and the coordinates of the centre of the circle, find the gradient of the radius joining these two points using the formula:

Gradient $= \frac{y_2 - y_1}{x_2 - x_1}$

Use this gradient to work out the gradient of the tangent, as these two lines are perpendicular to each other. If one line has a gradient m_1 and the other a gradient of m_2 then $m_1 m_2 = -1$.

NAILIT!

Remember, perpendicular means 'at right angles to'.

Use the coordinates of the point where the tangent touches the circle and the gradient of the tangent and substitute them into the following formula to give the equation of the tangent:

$$y - y_1 = m(x - x_1)$$

> You learned how to find the equation of a line from the gradient and a point on the line on page 37.

WORKIT!

A circle with equation $x^2 + y^2 = 25$ has centre O and a tangent to the circle at the point $P(3, 4)$.

a Find the gradient of the line OP.

Gradient of $OP = \dfrac{y_2 - y_1}{x_2 - x_1} = \dfrac{4 - 0}{3 - 0} = \dfrac{4}{3}$

b Using your answer to part a, write down the gradient of the tangent to the circle at point P.

As radius OP and tangent are perpendicular the product of their gradients is -1.

Gradient of tangent $= -\dfrac{3}{4}$

c Find the equation of the tangent passing through point P.

$y - y_1 = m(x - x_1)$

$y - 4 = -\dfrac{3}{4}(x - 3)$ ← Use this with $m = -\dfrac{3}{4}$ and $(x_1, y_1) = (3, 4)$.

$4y - 16 = -3x + 9$

$4y = -3x + 25$

DO IT!

Draw a flowchart for finding the equation of the tangent to a circle.

> The easiest way to find the gradient of the tangent is to invert the gradient of OP (put the fraction upside down) and change the sign.

✓ CHECKIT!

1 A circle has the equation $x^2 + y^2 = 49$.

  a Write down the coordinates of the centre of the circle.

  b Write down the radius of the circle.

2 The diagram shows a circle with centre at the origin O.

  a Find the equation of the circle.

A tangent to the circle is drawn at $(8, 6)$.

  b Write down the gradient of the tangent at this point.

  c Work out the equation of the tangent at $(8, 6)$.

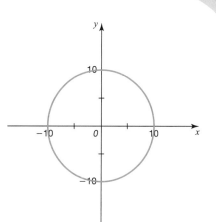

Real-life graphs

Distance–time graphs

These are the main features of any **distance–time graph**.

- Gradient of a line is the average speed. A steeper line means a higher speed.
- Horizontal sections mean the motion has stopped.
- A negative gradient shows the speed of the return journey.

Below is a distance–time graph for someone's journey to and from a meeting.

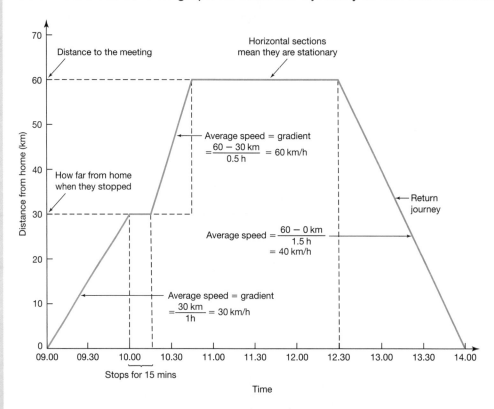

There are lots of things you can tell from this graph and some of them are marked on it. Other things you can tell include:

- The average speed in the first hour is lower than the average speed when they continued after stopping for 15 minutes.
- They stopped at 10 am and waited for 15 minutes.
- The meeting started at 10.45 am and finished at 12.30 pm so it took $1\frac{3}{4}$ hours.

Velocity–time graphs

These are the main features of a **velocity–time graph**.

- The gradient represents the acceleration. A positive gradient represents a positive acceleration and a negative gradient represents a negative acceleration (or deceleration). The units for acceleration are m/s².
- Horizontal sections represent constant velocity.
- The area under the graph represents the distance travelled.

DOIT!

Draw and annotate a distance–time graph of a journey to and from a friend's house.

STRETCHIT!

If the velocity–time graph is a curve, work out the distance travelled by dividing the area into strips. Find the area of each strip and then add them up. Alternatively, you can count the squares and multiply this number by the distance that is equivalent to one square.

If the graph is a curve, you can still find the acceleration.

WORKIT!

This velocity–time graph is for a car moving along a straight horizontal road. Its initial velocity is 20 m/s.

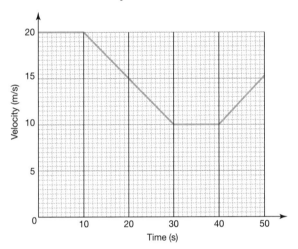

> Area of trapezium $= \frac{1}{2}$ (sum of the two parallel sides) × distance between them. Alternatively, divide the shape into a triangle and a rectangle and add the two areas together. Note you will not be given the formula for the area of a trapezium.

a Find the distance travelled while the car is decelerating.

Distance = area of trapezium ◄

$= \frac{1}{2}(20 + 10) \times 20$ ◄ Base of trapezium is when the car is decelerating, between 10 and 30 seconds.

$= 300$ m

> Sides of trapezium are the velocity before decelerating and the velocity after.

b Find the total distance travelled while travelling at constant speed.

Total distance while travelling at constant speed $= 20 \times 10 + 10 \times 10 = 300$ m ◄ Find areas of the rectangles where the car is travelling at constant speed.

c During the last stage of the motion the car accelerates. Calculate the acceleration.

Acceleration = gradient $= \dfrac{15 - 10}{10} = 0.5$ m/s^2

d Calculate the total distance travelled during the motion described by the graph.

Distance travelled while accelerating $= \frac{1}{2}(10 + 15) \times 10 = 125$ m

From a, b and d, total distance travelled $= 300 + 300 + 125$

$= 725$ m

> The total distance is the total area under the velocity–time graph.

Graphs in finance

Graphs are used in finance to show costs.

This graph shows how the cost of water varies with the volume used.

These are the key features of the graph:

- The intercept on the y-axis shows that there is a fixed cost when no water is used.

- Reading off the graph, the fixed charge is £34.

- The gradient of the graph is the cost per m³ of the water. The line goes through (50, 160) and (0, 34) so these points can be used to work out the cost per m³.

  Cost per m³ $= \dfrac{160 - 34}{50 - 0} = \dfrac{126}{50} =$ £2.52

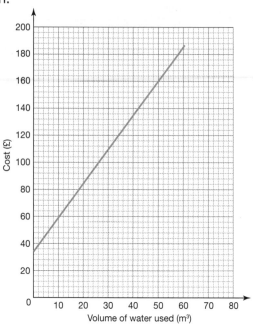

✓ CHECKIT!

1 The distance–time graph represents a cycle ride.

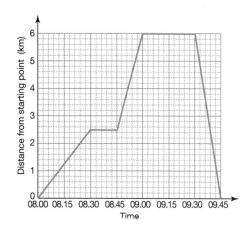

a Find the average speed for the first half-hour.

b At 08.30, the cyclists stopped for a break. How long was this break in hours?

c Find the average speed for the return journey.

2 A particle starts from rest and travels in a straight line. It accelerates uniformly for 2 s, then travels at a constant velocity of u m/s for 10 s, before decelerating uniformly to rest in 3 s. The total distance travelled by the particle is 50 m.

a Draw a velocity–time graph to show the motion of the particle.

b Find the value of u.

c Find the magnitude of the deceleration.

Generating sequences

Arithmetic and geometric sequences

An **arithmetic sequence** (sometimes called a linear sequence or an arithmetic progression) is a sequence of numbers with a constant difference (positive or negative) between each number and the one before. Add that same amount to give the next number in the sequence.

1, 3, 5, 7,…	Add 2 to get the next term.
13, 18, 23, 28,…	Add 5 to get the next term.
10, 6, 2, −2, −6,…	Add −4 (i.e. subtract 4) to get the next term.

WORKIT!

The first four terms of a sequence are 33, 30, 27, 24,…

a Write down the next two terms.

   21, 18 ◄

b What is the rule for continuing this sequence?

   Subtract 3

> The sequence goes down by 3 each time.

c What is the first negative number in this sequence?

   18, 15, 12, 9, 6, 3, 0, −3

   The first negative term is −3.

A **geometric sequence** (sometimes called a geometric progression) is a sequence of numbers with a constant ratio between each number and the one before. Multiply each number in the sequence by the same amount to give the next number in the sequence.

1, 3, 9, 27, 81,…	Multiply by 3 to get the next term.
$\frac{1}{2}, \frac{1}{4}, \frac{1}{8}, \frac{1}{16},…$	Multiply by $\frac{1}{2}$ to get the next term.
1, $\sqrt{3}$, 3, 3$\sqrt{3}$,…	Multiply by $\sqrt{3}$ to get the next term.

DOIT!

Summarise the difference between an arithmetic and a geometric sequence in 21 words.

Other common sequences

> A Fibonacci sequence usually starts 1, 1, but can start with any two numbers.

SNAPIT!   Common sequences

Sequence	Name	Rule
1, 4, 9, 16, 25, 36,…	Square numbers	Square the number of each term.
1, 8, 27, 64, 125, 216,…	Cube numbers	Cube the number of each term.
1, 3, 6, 10, 15, 21,…	Triangular numbers	As shown in the diagram on page 56.
1, 1, 2, 3, 5, 8,…	Fibonacci numbers	Add together the previous two terms. ◄

Triangular numbers

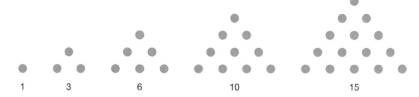

1   3   6   10   15

NAILIT!

Remember these common sequences, as they often come up in exam questions.

WORKIT!

Write down the next two terms in these sequences.

A geometric sequence with a ratio of 3 →

a $\frac{1}{9}, \frac{1}{3}, 1, 3,...$

　　9, 27

An arithmetic sequence with a common difference of −2 →

b 7, 5, 3, 1,...

　　−1, −3

c 1, 8, 27,...

　　64, 125 ← The cube numbers

d 1, 1, 2, 3, 5,...

　　8, 13 ← Fibonacci sequence

NAILIT!

Sometimes you will be given the rule and a term, and be asked to find the previous term. You need to use the inverse operations from the rule: for example, 'multiply by 2 and subtract 3' would become 'add 3 and divide by 2'. Note that you need to do the opposite operations and in the **opposite order**.

✓ CHECKIT!

1 Write down the next term of each of these sequences

　a 5, 8, 11, 14,...

　b 2.2, 2.4, 2.6, 2.8,...

　c 0, −3, −6, −9,...

　d 2, 12, 72,...

　e $\frac{1}{6}, \frac{1}{12}, \frac{1}{24},...$

　f $\frac{1}{2}, -\frac{1}{4}, \frac{1}{8},...$

2 The term-to-term rule for a sequence is square and add one. The first term of the sequence is −4. Find the 2nd and 3rd terms.

3 The term-to-term rule for a sequence is double and add one. The third term of the sequence is 12. Find the 1st and 2nd terms.

The *n*th term

The *n*th term of a sequence is a formula that gives the value of any term depending on its position in the sequence. For example, to find the 3rd term, put 3 into the formula.

The *n*th term of a linear sequence

To find the *n*th term of the linear sequence: 8, 13, 18, 23,…

n	1	2	3	4
Term	8	13	18	23
Difference		5	5	5

> Write the position of the term above the term.

> Find the difference between terms.

As there is a constant difference of 5 the first part of the formula will be 5*n*.

5*n*	5	10	15	20
Term − 5*n*	3	3	3	3

> Work out the difference between each term and 5*n*.

The *n*th term is 5*n* + 3.

> Sometimes you may have to subtract a value instead of add.

WORKIT!

Here are the first four terms of a sequence 2, 5, 8, 11,…

a Write an expression, in terms of *n*, for the *n*th term of the sequence.

n	1	2	3	4
Term	2	5	8	11
Difference		3	3	3
3*n*	3	6	9	12
Term − 3*n*	−1	−1	−1	−1

*n*th term = 3*n* − 1

b Find the 10th term in the sequence.

10th term = 3 × 10 − 1 = 29

> Substitute *n* = 10 into the formula for the 10th term.

c Is 200 a term of this sequence? Explain your answer.

$$3n - 1 = 200$$
$$3n = 201$$
$$n = 67$$

> Put the *n*th term formula equal to the term. If *n* works out as an integer, it is a number in the sequence.

As *n* is a whole number, 200 is a term in the sequence.

The nth term of a quadratic sequence

In a quadratic sequence the nth term includes a term in n^2.

To find the nth term for the sequence 4, 9, 16, 25,… first find the first and second differences between the terms:

Term	4		9		16		25
First difference		5		7		9	
Second difference			2		2		

> The second difference is the difference between successive first differences.

A constant second difference means that there must be an n^2 term. To find the number in front of n^2, divide the second difference by 2 (in this case, $2 \div 2 = 1$).

So the formula starts n^2. So we can summarise what we know:

n	1	2	3	4
Term	4	9	16	25
n^2	1	4	9	16
Term $- n^2$	3	5	7	9

> We know each term contains n^2. So work out the difference between each term and n^2.

Use the differences between this set of terms to work out the linear part of the sequence (the term in n).

Difference		2		2		2	
$2n$	2		4		6		8
Term $- n^2 - 2n$	1		1		1		1

> A difference of 2 means the linear part will start with $2n$.

Combining the terms gives nth term $= n^2 + 2n + 1$

DOIT!

Draw a flowchart for finding the nth term of a sequence. The chart needs to work with both arithmetic and quadratic sequences.

CHECKIT!

1 The nth term of a sequence is $50 - 3n$.

  a Write down the first three terms of this sequence.

  b Does the sequence contain the number 34?

  c Work out the value of the first term of this sequence that is negative.

2 The nth term of a sequence is given by 2×3^n.

  a Write down the first four terms of this sequence.

  b All the terms in this sequence are multiples of 6. Explain why.

3 The first four terms of an arithmetic sequence are -1, 1, 3, 5.

  a Work out an expression for the nth term of this sequence.

  b The xth term of this sequence has a value of 59. Find the value of x.

4 A sequence has the following first four terms:

4, 17, 38, 67

Find a formula for the nth term of this sequence.

Arguments and proofs

Arguments and proofs can crop up in almost any topic. As a result of this there is no set way of tackling them. The main thing to remember is that you have to sometimes put letters for values, angles, sides, and so on. Sometimes there are several ways to solve the problem.

WORKIT!

Here are four expressions

$x - 1$ $3x - 3$ $x^2 - 4$ $2(x + 1)$

x is a positive integer. Explain which expression has a value which is

a always even

   2 is a factor of $2(x + 1)$.

   So $2(x + 1)$ is always even.

b always a multiple of 3

   $3x - 3 = 3(x - 1)$, so 3 is a factor.

   So $3(x - 1)$ is always a multiple of 3.

c never zero.

   When $x = 1$, $x - 1 = 0$

   When $x = 1$, $3x - 3 = 0$

   When $x = 2$, $x^2 - 4 = 0$ ◄———

> Sometimes you can show something is **not** true by giving one **counter-example**.

   $2(x + 1)$ is always greater than zero, because x is always greater than 0.

   So $2(x + 1)$ is never zero.

WORKIT!

Prove that $(2x - 1)^2 - (x - 2)^2$ is a multiple of 3 for all integer values of x. ◄———

> Expand the brackets.

$(2x - 1)^2 - (x - 2)^2 = 4x^2 - 4x + 1 - (x^2 - 4x + 4)$

$= 4x^2 - 4x + 1 - x^2 + 4x - 4$

$= 3x^2 - 3$

$= 3(x^2 - 1)$ ◄———

> Factorise the expression.

The 3 outside the brackets shows that the result is a multiple of 3 for all integer values of x.

NAILIT!

If you are asked to prove something for even and/or odd numbers, use an expression of the form $2n$ for even numbers and $2n + 1$ for odd numbers.

WORKIT!

Prove that the product of two odd numbers always gives an answer that is odd.

Let two odd numbers be $2m + 1$ and $2n + 1$.

> $2n$ must be even, so $2n + 1$ must be odd.

Multiply the two expressions to find the product.

$(2m + 1)(2n + 1) = 4mn + 2m + 2n + 1$

$= 2(2mn + m + n) + 1$

Always state what you have been asked to prove at the end of your proof.

$2(2mn + m + n)$ must be even, so $2(2mn + m + n) + 1$ must be odd.

Therefore the product of two odd numbers is always an odd number.

CHECKIT!

1 Prove whether each of these statements is true or false.

   a If n is a positive integer, $2n + 1$ is always an odd number.

   b If $x^2 - 9 = 0$, the only value x can be is 3.

   c If $n > 0$, n^2 is always an integer.

   d If $n > 0$, n^2 is always greater than n.

2 Prove that the sum of four consecutive numbers is always even.

3 Prove that the sum of three consecutive integers is always a multiple of 3.

4 a and b are both integers and $a > b$. Prove whether each of these statements is true or false.

   a $\frac{a}{b} < 1$

   b $b^2 > a^2$

   c $\sqrt{a} > 1$

1 Multiply out the brackets and simplify where possible

  a $-3(3x - 4)$

  b $4x + 3(x + 2) - (x + 2)$

  c $(x + 3)(2x - 1)(3x + 5)$

2 **a** Factorise the expression $2x^2 + 7x - 4$.

  b Solve the equation $2x^2 + 7x - 4 = 0$.

3 Simplify

  a $(2x^2y)^3$ **c** $\dfrac{15a^3b}{3a^3b^2}$

  b $2x^{-3} \times 3x^4$

4 Solve the simultaneous equations

  $3x + 2y = 8$

  $5x + y = 11$

5 **a** Show that $\dfrac{3}{x + 7} = \dfrac{2 - x}{x + 1}$ can be written as $x^2 + 8x - 11 = 0$.

  b Hence solve the equation $\dfrac{3}{x + 7} = \dfrac{2 - x}{x + 1}$, giving your answers to 2 decimal places.

6 Make x the subject of $\dfrac{3y - x}{z} = ax + 2$.

7 The function f is such that $f(x) = \frac{x}{3} + 5$.

  a Find $f^{-1}(x)$.

  b The function g is such that $g(x) = 2x^2 + k$, where k is a constant.

    Given that $fg(2) = 10$, work out the value of k.

8 The nth term of a sequence is $30 - 4n$.

  a Write down the first three terms of this sequence.

  b Work out the value of the first term of this sequence that is negative.

9 A circle has the equation $x^2 + y^2 = 21$. Determine whether the point (4, 3) lies inside or outside this circle.

10 Simplify fully $(\sqrt{x} + \sqrt{9y})(\sqrt{x} - 3\sqrt{y})$.

11 **a** Write $2x^2 + 8x + 1$ in the form $a(x + b)^2 + c$, where a, b and c are integers.

  b Hence or otherwise, for the graph $y = 2x^2 + 8x + 1$:

    i find the coordinates of the turning point

    ii find the roots to 1 decimal place.

  c Sketch the graph of $y = 2x^2 + 8x + 1$.

12 The perimeters of rectangle $ABCD$ and triangle EFG are the same.

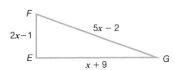

All measurements are in centimetres.

Work out the area of the triangle.

13 $A(-5, 2)$, $B(-2, -2)$, $C(2, 1)$ and $D(-1, k)$ are the vertices of a square.

  Find the equation of the diagonal BD.

14 Solve algebraically the simultaneous equations

  $x^2 + y^2 = 4$

  $2y - x = 2$

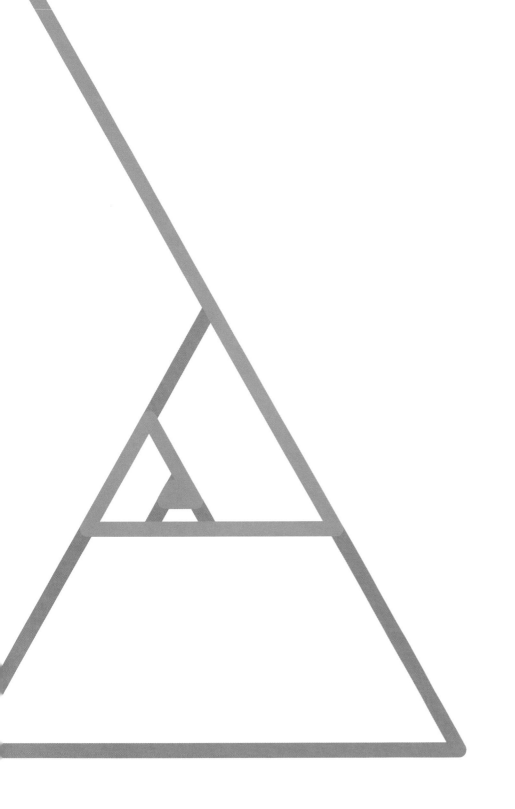

EXAM
PRACTICE

Algebra
Simple algebraic techniques

NAILIT!

Make sure you understand the difference between terms such as equation, expression, identity and formula.

(1) Identify whether each of these is a formula, expression, equation or identity. (★)

a $v^2 = u^2 + 2as$ (1 mark)

....

d $(2a^2b)^2 = 4a^4b^2$ (1 mark)

....

b $5x(2x + y) = 10x^2 + 5xy$ (1 mark)

....

e $P = I^2R$ (1 mark)

....

c $6a^2b$ (1 mark)

....

[Total: 5 marks]

NAILIT!

Collect together like terms, with identical letters and powers.

(2) Simplify $4x + 3x \times 2x - 3x$. (2 marks, ★★)

....

(3) Karl is trying to work out two values of y for which $y^3 - y = 0$.

The two values he finds are 1 and -1.

Are these two values correct? You must show your working. (3 marks, ★★★)

....

(4) Simplify these expressions. (★★★)

a $6x - (-4x)$
(1 mark)

b $x^2 - 2x - 4x + 3x^2$
(1 mark)

c $(-2x)^2 + 6x \times 3x - 4x^2$
(2 marks)

....

[Total: 4 marks]

(5) $s = \dfrac{v^2 - u^2}{2a}$ (★★★)

Work out the value of s when

a $v = 3$, $u = 1$ and $a = 2$
(1 mark)

b $v = -4$, $u = 3$ and $a = 4$
(1 mark)

c $v = 5$, $u = -2$ and $a = -7$
(1 mark)

....

[Total: 3 marks]

Removing brackets

① Expand the brackets for these expressions. (★)

   a $8(3x - 7)$ (1 mark)   **b** $-3(2x - 4)$ (1 mark)

.... **[Total: 2 marks]**

② Simplify (★★)

   a $3(2x - 1) - 3(x - 4)$ (2 marks)   **c** $5ab(2a - b)$ (2 marks)

....

   b $4y(2x + 1) + 6(x - y)$ (2 marks) **d** $x^2y^3(2x + 3y)$ (2 marks)

.... **[Total: 8 marks]**

③ Expand and simplify (★★★★)

   a $(m - 3)(m + 8)$ (2 marks)   **c** $(3x - 1)^2$ (2 marks)

....

   b $(4x - 1)(2x + 7)$ (2 marks)   **d** $(2x + y)(3x - y)$ (3 marks)

.... **[Total: 9 marks]**

④ Expand and simplify (★★★★)

   a $(x + 5)(x + 2)$ (2 marks)   **c** $(x - 7)(x + 1)$ (2 marks)

....

   b $(x + 4)(x - 4)$ (2 marks)   **d** $(3x + 1)(5x + 3)$ (2 marks)

.... **[Total: 8 marks]**

⑤ Expand and simplify (★★★★★)

   a $(x + 3)(x - 1)(x + 4)$ (3 marks)   **b** $(3x - 4)(2x - 5)(3x + 1)$ (3 marks)

.... **[Total: 6 marks]**

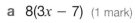

NAILIT!

Watch out for negative numbers outside the bracket as the signs will change when you multiply them out.

NAILIT!

Use the laws of indices when you expand brackets.

Factorising

① Factorise fully (★★★)

   a $25x^2 - 5xy$ (2 marks)

   b $4\pi r^2 + 6\pi x$ (2 marks)

   c $6a^3b^2 + 12ab^2$ (2 marks)

....

....

....

[Total: 6 marks]

WORKIT!

Factorise $15xy + 3x^2$.

> Take the common factors outside the brackets.

$15xy + 3x^2 = 3x(5y + x)$

SNAPIT! Factorising

> Factorising is the reverse process to expanding the brackets.

② Factorise (★★★)

   a $9x^2 - 1$ (2 marks)

....

> Use the difference of two squares:
>
> $a^2 - b^2 = (a + b)(a - b)$

   b $16x^2 - 4$ (2 marks)

....

[Total: 4 marks]

NAILIT!

Make sure that you take out all factors.

When a question says 'factorise fully', there is usually more than one factor. But if the question just says 'factorise' still check for more than one factor.

③ Factorise (★★★)

   a $a^2 + 12a + 32$ (2 marks)

   b $p^2 - 10p + 24$ (2 marks)

....

....

[Total: 4 marks]

WORKIT!

Factorise $x^2 - 2x - 8$.

> Find two numbers that multiply to make -8 and sum to make -2.

2 and -4

$x^2 - 2x - 8 = (x + 2)(x - 4)$

④ Factorise (★★★)

   a $a^2 + 12a$ (2 marks)

   c $x^2 - 11x + 30$ (2 marks)

....

....

   b $b^2 - 9$ (2 marks)

....

[Total: 6 marks]

(5) Factorise (★★★★★)

a $3x^2 + 20x + 32$ (3 marks)

c $2x^2 - x - 10$ (3 marks)

....

....

b $3x^2 + 10x - 13$ (3 marks)

....

[Total: 9 marks]

(6) Work out $\dfrac{x + 15}{2x^2 - 3x - 9} + \dfrac{3}{2x + 3}$.

Give your answer in its simplest form. (4 marks, ★★★★★)

....

(7) Write $\dfrac{1}{8x^2 - 2x - 1} \div \dfrac{1}{4x^2 - 4x + 1}$ in the form $\dfrac{ax + b}{cx + d}$ where a, b, c and d are integers.

(3 marks, ★★★★★)

....

Changing the subject of a formula

(1) Make T the subject of the formula $PV = nRT$. (2 marks, ★★)

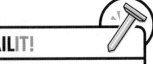

NAILIT!

To change the subject of a formula you have to get the subject on its own on one side of the equation.

....

(2) Make y the subject of the formula $2y + 4x - 1 = 0$. (2 marks, ★★★)

NAILIT!

Add, subtract, divide or multiply both sides by the same number, letter or combination of letters.

....

(3) Make a the subject of the formula $v = u + at$. (2 marks, ★★★)

....

(4) Make x the subject of the formula $y = \frac{x}{5} - m$. (2 marks, ★★★)

....

(5) Make v the subject of the formula $E = \frac{1}{2}mv^2$. (2 marks, ★★★)

....

(6) The volume of a cone is given by the formula $V = \frac{1}{3}\pi r^2 h$ where V is the volume, r is the radius and h is the perpendicular height. (★★★)

  a Rearrange the formula to make r the subject. (2 marks)

....

  b Find the radius of a cone with a volume of 100 cm³ and a height of 8 cm.
    Give your answer to 2 decimal places. (2 marks)

....

[Total: 4 marks]

(7) A straight line has the equation $y = 3x - 9$. (★★★)

a Rearrange the equation to make x the subject. (1 mark)

....

b Find the value of x when $y = 3$. (1 mark)

....

[Total: 2 marks]

(8) Make x the subject of $3y - x = ax + 2$. (4 marks, ★★★★)

NAILIT!

When the subject appears on both sides, first get the terms containing the subject on one side. Then collect like terms or factorise to make sure the subject only appears once.

....

(9) a Make c the subject of the formula $c^2 = \dfrac{(16a^2 b^4 c^2)^{\frac{1}{2}}}{4a^2 b}$.

(2 marks, ★★★★★)

....

b $a = 2.8$ and $b = 3.2$, both to 1 decimal place. (3 marks, ★★★★★)

Work out the upper and lower bounds of c. Give your answers to 3 significant figures.

....

[Total: 5 marks]

Solving linear equations

1 Solve these equations. (★★)

a $2x + 11 = 25$ (1 mark)

....

b $3x - 5 = 10$ (1 mark)

....

c $15x = 60$ (1 mark)

....

d $\frac{x}{4} = 8$ (1 mark)

....

e $\frac{4x}{5} = 20$ (1 mark)

....

f $\frac{2x}{3} = -6$ (1 mark)

....

g $5 - x = 7$ (1 mark)

....

h $\frac{x}{7} - 9 = 3$ (1 mark)

....

NAILIT!

To solve a linear equation with only one unknown value perform the same operation(s) to both sides (add, subtract, multiply or divide) to get the unknown value on its own on one side.

[Total: 8 marks]

2 Solve the equation $5x - 1 = 2x + 1$. (2 marks, ★★)

....

3 Solve the equations. (★★★)

a $\frac{1}{4}(2x - 1) = 3(2x - 1)$ (3 marks)

....

b $5(3x + 1) = 2(5x - 3) + 3$ (3 marks)

....

[Total: 6 marks]

Solving quadratic equations using factorisation

WORKIT!

Solve $x^2 - 2x - 2 = 2x + 3$.

1 Rewrite the equation as a quadratic equal to zero.

$x^2 - 4x - 5 = 0$

2 Factorise.

$(x - 5)(x + 1) = 0$

3 Set each bracket equal to zero.

$x - 5 = 0$ or $x + 1 = 0$

$x = 5$ or $x = -1$

NAILIT!

Make sure you can expand brackets and factorise before attempting these questions.

NAILIT!

Remember that a quadratic must be equal to zero before you can factorise and hence solve it.

(1) **a** Factorise $x^2 - 7x + 12$. (2 marks, ★★★)

....

b Solve $x^2 - 7x + 12 = 0$. (1 mark, ★★★)

....

[Total: 3 marks]

(2) **a** Factorise $2x^2 + 5x - 3$. (3 marks, ★★★★)   **b** Solve $2x^2 + 5x - 3 = 0$. (1 mark, ★★★)

NAILIT!

You need to recognise quadratic expressions that can be factorised into two brackets.

....

[Total: 4 marks]

(3) Solve the equation $x^2 - 3x - 20 = x - 8$. (4 marks, ★★★★)

....

4 **a** Show that the equation $x(x - 8) - 7 = x(5 - x)$ can be rearranged to
$2x^2 - 13x - 7 = 0$. (2 marks, ★★★★)

NAILIT!

If a quadratic equation appears in a problem, always check whether both solutions are possible or only one of them.

b Hence find the solutions to $x(x - 8) - 7 = x(5 - x)$. (3 marks, ★★★★)

....

[Total: 5 marks]

5 The diagram shows a trapezium with the sides measured in cm.

The trapezium has an area of $16 \, \text{cm}^2$.

Find the value of x. (4 marks, ★★★★★)

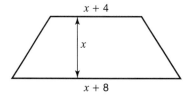

NAILIT!

Area of a trapezium
$= \frac{1}{2}(a + b)h$
where a and b are the lengths of the two parallel sides and h is the distance between them.

....

Solving quadratic equations using the formula

(1) **a** Show that $\frac{3}{x+7} = \frac{2-x}{x+1}$ can be written as $x^2 + 8x - 11 = 0$.

(3 marks, ★★★★★)

....

b Hence solve the equation $\frac{3}{x+7} = \frac{2-x}{x+1}$.

Give your answers to 2 decimal places. (2 marks, ★★★★★)

NAILIT!

Quadratic equations of the form $ax^2 + bx + c = 0$ $(a \neq 0)$ can be solved using the formula

$$x = \frac{-b + \sqrt{b^2 - 4ac}}{2a}$$

NAILIT!

Be careful with the signs when entering numbers into the formula. If you end up with the square root of a negative number you have made a mistake.

[Total: 5 marks]

(2) The right-angled triangle shown has an area of 40 cm². All measurements are in centimetres. (5 marks, ★★★★★)

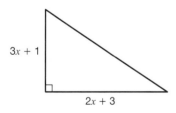

$3x + 1$

$2x + 3$

Find the value of x to 2 decimal places.

....

(3) Calculate the x-coordinates of the points of intersection of the line $y = x - 8$ and the curve $y = x^2 - 2x - 9$. Give your answers to 2 decimal places. (5 marks, ★★★★★)

NAILIT!

If you are asked to solve a quadratic equation giving your answer to a certain number of decimal places then you probably need to use the formula.

....

Solving simultaneous equations

1 Solve these simultaneous equations algebraically.

$2x - 3y = -5$

$5x + 2y = 16$ (3 marks, ★★★)

> The opposite signs for the y terms mean that it is easier to make these terms the same in value but opposite in sign and add the two equations.

NAILIT!

You can solve simultaneous equations:
- graphically, by finding where the equations intersect on a graph
- by eliminating one of the unknowns by adding or subtracting the equations
- by substituting the expression for one variable into the other equation.

NAILIT!

Be careful with the signs when solving simultaneous equations using the elimination method, especially if you have to subtract one equation from the other.

$x = $ .... $y = $ ....

2 **a** Plot the graph of $y = 3x - 2$ on the set of axes given. (2 marks, ★★★)

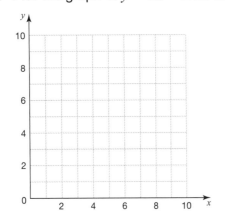

NAILIT!

Only use x values that are on the graph and check that the resulting y values will fit on the graph. You only need two points to plot a straight line, but plotting three points means that you can identify whether you have made a mistake.

b Hence solve the pair of simultaneous equations (3 marks, ★★★)

$y = 3x - 2$

$y = 10 - x$

$x = $ .... $y = $ ....

[Total: 5 marks]

3 Solve these simultaneous equations.

$x - y = 3$

$x^2 + y^2 = 9$ (5 marks, ★★★★★)

NAILIT!

If one of the equations is a circle or a quadratic, you must use the substitution method or draw the graphs.

$x = $ .... $y = $ ....

Solving inequalities

(1) Solve these inequalities. (★★★)

a $\dfrac{x + 5}{4} \geq -1$

(1 mark)

b $3x - 4 > 4x + 8$

(2 marks)

 **NAILIT!**

Solve inequalities in the same way as ordinary equations, except that if you multiply or divide by a negative number, reverse the inequality sign.

....

[Total: 3 marks]

(2) Show the inequality $-3 < x \leq 2$ on the number line below. (2 marks, ★★)

$$\underset{\substack{-4 \ \ -3 \ \ -2 \ \ -1 \ \ \ 0 \ \ \ 1 \ \ \ 2 \ \ \ 3 \ \ \ 4}}{\longmapsto} x$$

(3) **a** Use the grid to shade the region represented by these inequalities. (5 marks, ★★★★★)

$x \leq 1 \quad y > -2 \quad y - 2x < 1$

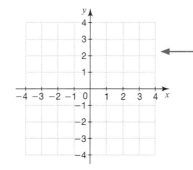

Show $<$ or $>$ with a dotted line, and $\leq$ or $\geq$ with a solid line. Shade inside the region enclosed by the lines.

b List the integer values of coordinates that satisfy all of these inequalities. (2 marks, ★★★★★)

....

[Total: 7 marks]

(4) Solve the inequality $x^2 + 2x \leq 3$. (5 marks, ★★★★★)

....

(5) Solve the inequality $x^2 - 2x - 15 > 0$. (5 marks, ★★★★★)

 **NAILIT!**

To solve a quadratic inequality, replace the inequality with $=$ and solve the equation. Sketch the graph to work out which values of x satisfy the inequality.

....

Problem solving using algebra

1. The length of a rectangular patio is 1 m more than its width.

   The perimeter of the patio is 26 m. Find the area of the patio. (3 marks, ★★★)

   NAILIT!

   Look for all the algebraic techniques when solving problems. You will often need to substitute letters for unknown values.

   ....

2. The cost of 2 adults' tickets and 5 children's tickets at a circus is £35.

   The cost of 3 adults' tickets and 4 children's tickets is £38.50.

   Find the cost of each type of ticket. (3 marks, ★★★★)

   ....

3. Rachel and Hannah are sisters.

   The product of their ages is 63. In two years' time, the product of their ages will be 99. (★★★★★)

   a Find the sum of their ages. (3 marks)

   ....

   b Rachel is 2 years older than Hannah. How old is Rachel? (2 marks)

   ....

   [Total: 5 marks]

Use of functions

(1) $f(x) = 5x + 4$ (★★)

   a Find f(3). (1 mark)

....

   b Find the value of x for which $f(x) = -1$. (2 marks)

....

[Total: 3 marks]

NAILIT!

If $f(x) = x^2 - 1$,
to find f(1) substitute $x = 1$:
$f(1) = 1^2 - 1 = 0$.

STRETCHIT!

If $f(x) = x^2 = y$, can you express x as a function of y, f(y)?

(2) If $f(x) = x^2$ and $g(x) = x - 6$, find (★★★)

   a fg(x) (1 mark)   **b** gf(x) (2 marks) ◄

> Apply the function nearest the x first and then apply the second function to the answer fg(x) = f(g(x)).

....

[Total: 3 marks]

(3) $f(x) = \sqrt{x + 4}$, where $x > -4$

   $g(x) = 2x^2 - 3$ for all values of x (★★★★)

   a Find f(5). (1 mark)   **b** Find an expression for gf(x).
                                     Simplify your answer. (2 marks)

....

[Total: 3 marks]

(4) $f(x) = 5x^2 + 3$

   Find $f^{-1}(x)$. (3 marks, ★★★★★)

NAILIT!

$f^{-1}(x)$ is the inverse of f(x).

....

Iterative methods

1 Show that the equation

$2x^3 - 2x + 1 = 0$

has a solution between -1 and -1.5. (3 marks, ★★★★)

> ### NAILIT!
> Iterative methods can be used to solve equations that are difficult to solve using other methods. They can also be used to show that a solution to an equation lies between two values.

> ### NAILIT!
> If f(x) can take any value between a and b, then if there is a change of sign between f(a) and f(b), a root of f(x) = 0 lies between a and b.

2 A sequence is generated using the iterative formula

 $x_{n+1} = x_n^3 + \frac{1}{9}$.

Starting with $x_0 = 0.1$, find x_1, x_2, x_3. For each of these, write down your full calculator display. (3 marks, ★★★★★)

$x_1 =$ ....

$x_2 =$ ....

$x_3 =$ ....

3 The cubic equation $x^3 - x - 2 = 0$ has a root α between 1 and 2. (★★★★★)

 The iterative formula

$x_{n+1} = (x_n + 2)^{\frac{1}{3}}$

with $x_0 = 1.5$, can be used to find α.

a Calculate x_4. Give your answer to 3 decimal places. (4 marks)

$x_4 =$ ....

b Prove that this value is also the value of α correct to 3 decimal places. (2 marks)

[Total: 6 marks]

(4) **a i** Sketch the graphs of $y = x^3$ and $y = 3 - x$. (2 marks, ★★★★★)

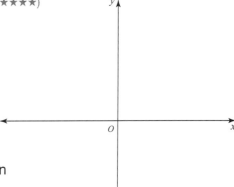

ii Hence write down the number of roots of the equation
$x^3 + x - 3 = 0$. (1 mark, ★★★★★)

....

b The cubic equation $x^3 + x - 3 = 0$ has a root α between 1 and 2.

The iterative formula
$$x_{n+1} = (3 - x_n)^{\frac{1}{3}}$$
with $x_0 = 1.2$, can be used to find α. Calculate x_6. Give your answer to 4 decimal places. (3 marks)

$x_6 = $ ....

[Total: 6 marks]

Equation of a straight line

(1) One of these graphs has the equation $y = 3 - 2x$.

State the letter of the correct graph. (1 mark, ★)

....

A 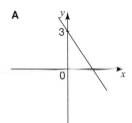 **B** 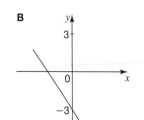 **C** 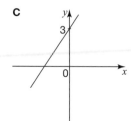 **D**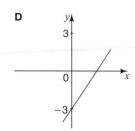

(2) **a** The line AB cuts the x-axis at 3 and the y-axis at 4.

Find the gradient of line AB. (2 marks, ★)

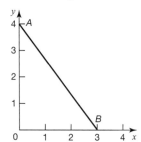

NAILIT!

The gradient of a straight line, $m = \dfrac{\text{change in } y\text{-values}}{\text{change in } x\text{-values}}$

The gradient of the line joining points (x_1, y_1) and (x_2, y_2) is given by $\dfrac{y_2 - y_1}{x_2 - x_1}$.

....

A straight line passes through the points $C(-3, 5)$ and $D(5, 1)$.

b Find the equation of line CD. (3 marks, ★★★★)

NAILIT!

Equations of straight lines are of the form $y = mx + c$, where m is the gradient (i.e. the steepness of the line) and c is the intercept on the y-axis.

Rearrange the equation so that it is in the form $y = mx + c$. Find the gradient and the intercept on the y-axis.

....

NAILIT!

The equation of a straight line with gradient m and which passes through point (x_1, y_1) is given by $y - y_1 = m(x - x_1)$.

c The midpoint of *CD* is *M*. A straight line is drawn through point *M* which is perpendicular to the line *CD*.

Find the equation of this line. (3 marks, ★★★★)

....

[Total: 8 marks]

(3) The gradient of line *OP* is 3. Its length is 12. (4 marks, ★★★★)

Find the coordinates of point *P*.
Give each coordinate to 1 decimal place.

You will need to use Pythagoras' theorem.

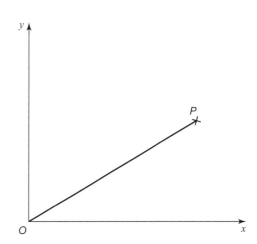

....

> **NAILIT!**
>
> When two lines are perpendicular to each other, the product of their gradients is −1.

Quadratic graphs

① **a** Using the method of completing the square, solve this quadratic equation.

Give your answers to 1 decimal place.

$x^2 + 4x + 1 = 0$ (4 marks, ★★★★★)

SNAPIT! **Quadratic graphs**

Quadratic graphs are ∪-shaped if the coefficient of x^2 is positive and ∩-shaped if the coefficient is negative.

....

b Hence sketch the graph of $y = x^2 + 4x + 1$ on the axes provided, including the coordinates of the turning point. (3 marks, ★★★★★)

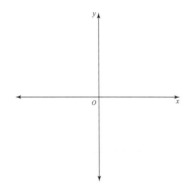

NAILIT!

To find the turning point of a quadratic graph, first complete the square to get the equation in the form $y = a(x + p)^2 + q$.

The turning point is at $(-p, q)$.

[Total: 7 marks]

② Express $5x^2 - 20x + 10$ in the form $a(x + b)^2 + c$.

Write down the values of a, b and c. (4 marks, ★★★★)

You will need to take 5 out as a factor as part of the process of completing the square.

....

③ Express $2x^2 + 12x + 3$ in the form $a(x + b)^2 + c$.

Write down the values of a, b and c. (4 marks, ★★★★)

....

Recognising and sketching graphs of functions

NAILIT!

You need to be familiar with the shapes of linear, quadratic, cubic, reciprocal, exponential and trigonometric functions. You need to know where the graphs intersect the axes as well as the shape.

① Fill in the table by inserting the letter of the graph that fits with the equation. (6 marks, ★★★★)

Equation	Graph
$y = x^2$	
$y = 2^x$	
$y = \sin x°$	
$y = x^3$	
$y = x^2 - 6x + 8$	
$y = \cos x°$	

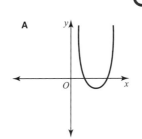
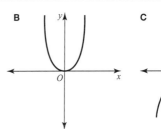
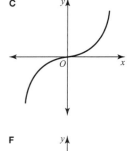
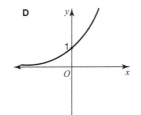
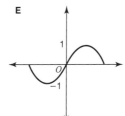
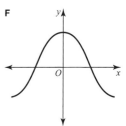

② a On the axes provided, sketch the graph of $y = \sin x$ for $0° \le x \le 360°$. (3 marks, ★★★★)

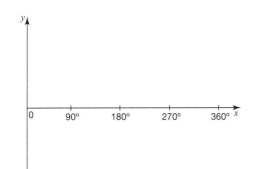

There is no scale on the y-axis. You need to mark the maximum and minimum values on the axis.

b On the axes provided, sketch the graph of $y = \tan x$ for $0° \le x \le 360°$. (3 marks, ★★★★)

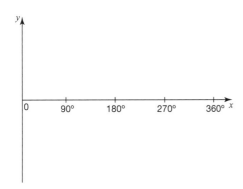

[Total: 6 marks]

③ Find all the values of θ in the range $0° \le \theta \le 360°$ that satisfy

$3\cos\theta = 1$.

Give your answers to 1 decimal place. (3 marks, ★★★★★)

Translations and reflections of functions

NAILIT!

$y = f(x) \rightarrow f(x + a)$:
translation of $-a$ units parallel to the x-axis

$y = f(x) \rightarrow f(x) + a$:
translation of a units parallel to the y-axis

$y = f(x) \rightarrow -f(x)$:
reflection in the x-axis

$y = f(x) \rightarrow f(-x)$:
reflection in the y-axis

---

(1) The quadratic curve $y = f(x)$ passes through the origin and the point (4, 0), and has a turning point at (2, −4). On the same axes, sketch the graphs of (★★★★)

a $y = -f(x)$ (2 marks)   **b** $y = f(x - 2)$ (2 marks)

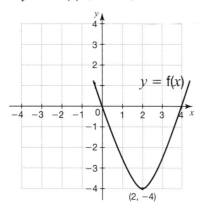

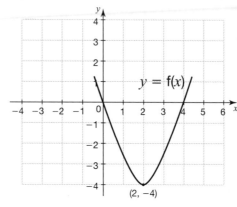

In each case, give the coordinates of the points of intersection of the graph with the x-axis and the coordinates of the turning point.

NAILIT!

A turning point is a maximum or minimum point on the curve.

....   **[Total: 4 marks]**

(2) The graph of $y = f(x)$ is shown on the right.

On the same axes, sketch the graphs of these functions. (★★★★)

a $y = -f(x)$ (2 marks)   **c** $y = f(-x)$ (2 marks)

b $y = f(x) + 2$ (2 marks)

[Total: 6 marks]

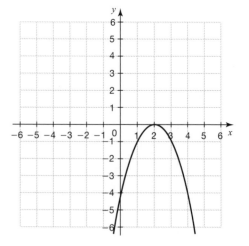

(3) On the axes below, sketch the graph of $y = \cos(x) + 2$ for $0° \leq x \leq 360°$. (2 marks, ★★★★★)

Equation of a circle and tangent to a circle

NAILIT!

A circle with centre the origin $(0, 0)$ and radius r has the equation $x^2 + y^2 = r^2$.

(1) Write down the radius of each of these circles. (★★★)

a $x^2 + y^2 = 25$ (1 mark)   **b** $x^2 + y^2 - 49 = 0$ (1 mark)   **c** $4x^2 + 4y^2 = 16$ (2 marks)

....

[Total: 4 marks]

(2) A circle has the equation $x^2 + y^2 = 21$. Determine whether the point $(4, 3)$ lies inside or outside this circle. (4 marks, ★★★★★)

> Compare the length of the line joining the origin to the point $(4, 3)$ with the radius of the circle.

....

(3) The point $P(5, 7)$ lies on a circle with centre the origin. (★★★★★)

a Find the radius of the circle.
Give your answer as a surd. (2 marks)

WORKIT!

The point $P(2, 3)$ lies on a circle with centre the origin, O.

Find the equation of the tangent to the circle at the point.

1 Find the gradient of the radius OP. $\frac{3}{2}$

2 Find the gradient of the tangent at P. $-\frac{2}{3}$

3 Use $y - y_1 = m(x - x_1)$.

$y - 3 = -\frac{2}{3}(x - 2)$ so

$y = -\frac{2}{3}x + \frac{13}{3}$

....

b Write down the equation of the circle. (1 mark)

....

c Find the equation of the tangent to the circle at point P. (3 marks)

NAILIT!

A tangent is a line which just touches the circle.

....

[Total: 6 marks]

Real-life graphs

1 The velocity–time graph shows the motion of an object. (★★★)

a Calculate the acceleration of the object during the first 10 seconds.
(2 marks)

....

b Calculate the total distance travelled by the object. (2 marks)

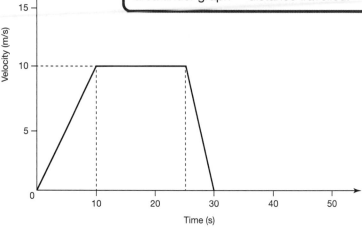

NAILIT!

In a distance–time graph,
gradient = velocity (or speed).

In a velocity–time (or speed–time) graph,
gradient = acceleration
area under graph = distance travelled.

....

[Total: 4 marks]

2 This is the speed–time graph for a car journey. (★★★★)

a Describe the motion of the car during the first 6 seconds. (1 mark)

....

b Describe the motion of the car between points *A* and *B* on the graph. (1 mark)

....

....

c Work out an estimate for the distance travelled by the car between points *A* and *B* on the graph by using three trapeziums. Give your answer to the nearest integer. (3 marks)

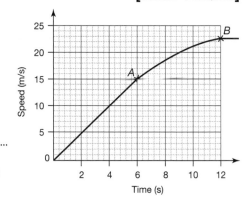

NAILIT!

To estimate the area under a curve, divide the area into trapeziums.

....

d Giving a reason, say whether your answer for the distance is an underestimate or an overestimate of the actual distance. (2 marks)

....

....

[Total: 7 marks]

Generating sequences

① **a** Work out the next term in each of these sequences. (★★)

　　i 16, 8, 4, 2, 1, ... (1 mark)　　**iii** 5, 9, 13, 17, ... (1 mark)

....　　　..

　　ii 3, 9, 27, 81, ... (1 mark)

....

b The following sequence is an arithmetic sequence.

Work out the missing two terms. (★★)

27, ..., ..., −12 (2 marks)

....

[Total: 5 marks]

② The first two terms of a sequence are

3, 1, ..., ...

The term-to-term rule for this sequence is to multiply the previous term by 2 and subtract 5.

Work out the next two terms of the sequence. (2 marks, ★★)

.... , ...

③ Write down the next two terms for these sequences. (★★★)

a 1, 4, 9, 16, ..., ... (1 mark)

.... , ...

b 1, 3, 6, 10, ..., ... (1 mark)

.... , ...

c 1, 1, 2, 3, 5, ..., ... (1 mark)

.... , ...

[Total: 3 marks]

NAILIT!

You need to be familiar with arithmetic and geometric sequences, as well as the sequences of square numbers, cube numbers, triangular numbers and Fibonacci numbers.

Look for adding or subtracting the same number to get from one term to the next. Then look for multiplying or dividing by the same number.

Work out the difference between 27 and −12. Then divide your answer by three, because three equal distances give two new terms (in the gaps between them).

NAILIT!

A term-to-term rule tells you how to work out the next term in the sequence from the current term.

First work out the difference between the two terms you are given.

NAILIT!

Not all sequences have a constant difference or multiplier. Try squares, cubes, triangular numbers and Fibonacci sequences.

The nth term

1 The first four terms of an arithmetic sequence are

2, 6, 10, 14, ... (★★★)

NAILIT!

You need to be able to write the nth term of linear and quadratic sequences as an expression containing n.

   a Find an expression for the nth term of this sequence. (2 marks)

....

   b Use your answer to part a to explain why all the terms of this sequence are even. (2 marks)

....

....

   c Work out whether 236 is a number in this sequence. (2 marks) ← Write 236 equal to the nth term.

....

[Total: 6 marks]

2 An expression for the nth term of a sequence is $9 - n^2$. (★★★)

   a Find the 2nd term of this sequence.
      (1 mark)

   c Explain why 10 cannot be a term in this sequence. (1 mark)

....

....

   b Find the 20th term of this sequence. (1 mark)

....

....

[Total: 3 marks]

3 Find the nth term for the sequence

1, 1, 3, 7, 13, ... ←

(5 marks, ★★★★★)

There is no constant difference here, so it is likely that this is a quadratic sequence. You need to find the 1st and 2nd differences.

WORKIT!

Find the nth term of the sequence   2   3   8   17 ...

1 Work out the 1st differences.   1   5   9

2 Work out the 2nd differences.   4   4

3 The coefficient of n^2 is $\frac{1}{2}$ × 2nd difference.

nth term starts $2n^2$

4 Subtract $2n^2$ from each term.   0   −5   −10   −15

5 Work out the nth term for sequence in step 4. $-5n + 5$

6 Combine the two expressions from steps 4 and 5.

nth term is $2n^2 - 5n + 5$.

....

Arguments and proofs

(1) Sarah says that all prime numbers are odd. By giving a counter-example, show that her statement is false. (1 mark, ★★)

....

NAILIT!

Proof questions can be on many topics but the majority of them can be solved algebraically. Often you need to substitute a letter to prove an expression. Sometimes you can prove something is not true by giving a counter-example (i.e. a situation when it is false).

(2) Explain whether each of these statements is true or false. (★★★)

a If n is a positive integer, $2n + 1$ is always greater than or equal to 3. (1 mark)

....

....

b $3(n + 1)$ is always a multiple of 3. (1 mark)

....

....

c If n is a positive integer, $2n - 3$ is always even. (1 mark)

....

....

[Total: 3 marks]

(3) Prove that the sum of any two consecutive integers is always an odd number. (3 marks, ★★★★)

> Start by letting the first number be x. Then write an expression in terms of x for the second number.

(4) Prove that $(2x - 1)^2 - (x - 2)^2$ is a multiple of 3 for all integer values of x. (3 marks, ★★★★★)

> Multiply out the brackets and then simplify. Look for a factor of 3.

(5) Prove that the difference between the squares of two consecutive odd numbers is always a multiple of 8. (5 marks, ★★★★★)

Answers

For full worked solutions, visit:
www.scholastic.co.uk/gcse

Revision answers

Simple algebraic techniques p.7

1 a formula **b** identity **c** expression
   d identity **e** equation
2 a $10x^2 + 4x$ **c** $-3x^2 + 10xy$
   b $3a - b$ **d** $3x^3 - x - 5$
3 16
4 4

Removing brackets p.10

1 a $2x + 8$ **c** $x - 1$ **e** $3x^2 + 3x$
   b $63x + 21$ **d** $3x^2 - x$ **f** $20x^2 - 8x$
2 a $5x + 12$ **c** $4x^2 + 2x$
   b $3x + 45$ **d** $3x^2 - 10x + 8$
3 a $t^2 + 8t + 15$ **c** $6y^2 + 41y + 63$
   b $x^2 - 9$ **d** $4x^2 - 4x + 1$
4 a $2x^3 + 21x^2 + 55x + 42$
   b $24x^3 - 46x^2 + 29x - 6$

Factorising p.13

1 a $6(4t + 3)$ **c** $5y(x + 3z)$
   b $a(9 - 2b)$ **d** $6xy^2(4x^2 + 1)$
2 a $(x + 7)(x + 3)$ **c** $(2x + 5)(3x + 2)$
   b $(x + 5)(x - 3)$ **d** $(2x + 7)(2x - 7)$
3 $\frac{1}{2x + 3}$

Changing the subject of a formula p.15

1 a $r = \sqrt{\frac{A}{\pi}}$ **b** $r = \sqrt{\frac{A}{4\pi}}$ **c** $r = \sqrt[3]{\frac{3V}{4\pi}}$
2 a $c = y - mx$ **d** $s = \frac{v^2}{2a}$
   b $u = v - at$ **e** $u = \sqrt{v^2 - 2as}$
   c $a = \frac{v-u}{t}$ **f** $t = \frac{2s}{u + v}$

Solving linear equations p.17

1 a $x = 3$ **b** $x = 3$ **c** $x = 20$
2 a $x = 5$ **b** $x = 18$ **c** $x = 20$
3 a $x = -2$ **b** $m = 1$ **c** $x = \frac{6}{5}, 1\frac{1}{5}$ or 1.2

Solving quadratic equations using factorisation p.19

1 a $x = -2$ or $x = -3$
   b $x = -3$ or $x = 4$
   c $x = -\frac{7}{2}$ or $x = -5$
2 a Area $= \frac{1}{2} \times$ base $\times$ height
       $\frac{1}{2}(2x + 3)(x + 4) = 9$
       $\frac{1}{2}(2x^2 + 11x + 12) = 9$
        $2x^2 + 11x + 12 = 18$
        $2x^2 + 11x - 6 = 0$
   b $x = \frac{1}{2}$ **c** base = 4 cm, height = 4.5 cm

3 By Pythagoras' theorem $(x + 1)^2 + (x + 8)^2 = 13^2$
   $x^2 + 2x + 1 + x^2 + 16x + 64 = 169$
   $2x^2 + 18x - 104 = 0$
   Dividing through by 2 gives
   $x^2 + 9x - 52 = 0$
   $(x - 4)(x + 13) = 0$
   So $x = 4$ or -13 (disregard $x = -13$ as x is a length)
   Hence $x = 4$ cm

Solving quadratic equations using the formula p.21

1 $x = 2.14$ or $x = -1.64$ (to 3 s.f.)
2 a $\frac{2x + 3}{x + 2} = 3x + 1$
        $2x + 3 = (3x + 1)(x + 2)$
        $2x + 3 = 3x^2 + 7x + 2$
         $0 = 3x^2 + 5x - 1$
      $3x^2 + 5x - 1 = 0$
   b $x = -1.85$ or $x = 0.18$ (to 2 d.p.)

Solving simultaneous equations p.24

1 a $x = 2, y = -1$
   b $x = 4, y = 2$
2 $x = \frac{1}{5}, y = -2\frac{3}{5}$ or $x = \frac{1}{2}, y = -2$
3 Equating the y values gives
   $x^2 + 5x - 4 = 6x + 2$
   $x^2 - x - 6 = 0$
   $(x - 3)(x + 2) = 0$
   $x = 3$ or -2
   When $x = 3, y = 6 \times 3 + 2 = 20$
   When $x = -2, y = 6 \times (-2) + 2 = -10$
   Points are (3, 20) and (-2, -10)

Solving inequalities p.28

1 a $x > 6$
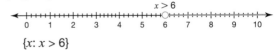
   $\{x: x > 6\}$
   b $x \geq 11$

   $\{x: x \geq 11\}$
   c $x < 26$

$\{x: x < 26\}$
2 a $x > 10$ **b** $x < 0.4$ or $\frac{2}{5}$ **c** $x \leq 8$

3 a

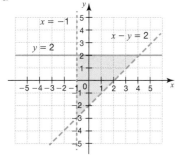

b (0, 2), (0,1), (0, 0), (0, −1), (1, 2), (1, 1), (1, 0), (2, 2), (2, 1), (3, 2)

4 $x < -2$ and $x > 5$

Problem solving using algebra p.30

1 26, 51   **2** 65   **3** 9 cm by 3 cm

Use of functions p.32

1 a −1   **b** $-\frac{2}{3}$ **c** $\frac{x+1}{x}$

2 a $\sqrt{x^2 + 8x + 7}$ **c** 4

   b $\sqrt{(x^2 - 9)} + 4$

Iterative methods p.34

1 1.521

Let $f(x) = x^3 - x - 2$

$f(1.5215) = (1.5215)^3 - 1.5215 - 2 = 0.0007151$

$f(1.5205) = (1.5205)^3 - 1.5205 - 2 = -0.005225$

As there is a change in sign, $a = 1.521$ to 3 decimal places.

Equation of a straight line p.38

1 a 2   **b** $-\frac{1}{2}$ **c** $y = -\frac{1}{2}x + 5$

2 $y = 3x - 3$

3 $2x - y + 2 = 0$

4 a $\frac{1}{2}$ **b** (2, 2)   **c** **i** −2

                                ii $y = -2x + 6$

Quadratic graphs p.42

1 a $2(x - 3)^2 - 17$ **c**

   b **i** (3, −17)

       ii $x = 0.1$ and $x = 5.9$

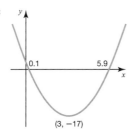

2 a $y = x^2 - 4x - 5$ **b** $y = -x^2 + 9x - 14$

3 a $x^2 + 12x - 16 = (x + 6)^2 - 52$

   b (−6, −52)

Recognising and sketching graphs of functions p.46

1 a B   **c** E   **e** D

   b F   **d** A   **f** C

2 a

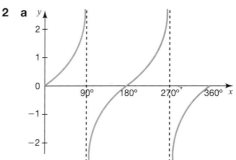

   b $x = 240°$

3 a A   **b** G   **c** F   **d** E

Translations and reflections of functions p.49

1 a (3, 5)   **c** (2, −5)

   b (−1, 5)   **d** (−2, 5)

2 a

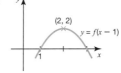

   c

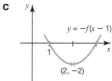

   b

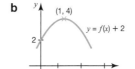

   d

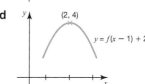

Equation of a circle and tangent to a circle p.51

1 a (0, 0)   **b** 7

2 a $x^2 + y^2 = 100$

   b Gradient of radius to (8, 6) = $\frac{6}{8} = \frac{3}{4}$

     Gradient of tangent = $-\frac{4}{3}$

   c $y = -\frac{4}{3}x + 16\frac{2}{3}$

Real-life graphs p.54

1 a 5 km/h   **b** 0.25 hours   **c** 24 km/h

2 a

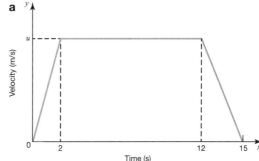

   b $u = 4$ m/s   **c** 1.33 m/s²

Generating sequences p.56

1 **a** 17   **c** −12   **e** $\frac{1}{48}$
  b 3.0   **d** 432   **f** $-\frac{1}{16}$

2 17, 290

3 2.25, 5.5

The *n*th term p.58

1 **a** 47, 44, 41
  b no   **c** −1

2 **a** 6, 18, 54, 162
  b Both 2 and 3 are factors, so 6 must also be a factor.

3 **a** *n*th term = $2n - 3$ **b** $x = 31$

4 *n*th term = $4n^2 + n - 1$

Arguments and proofs p.60

1 **a** True: $2n$ is always even as it is a factor of 2. Adding 1 to an even number always gives an odd number.
  b False: $x^2 = 9$, so $x = \sqrt{9} = \pm3$.
  c False: n could be a decimal such as 4.25, so squaring it would not give an integer.
  d False: if $n \leq 1$ this is not true.

2 Let the four consecutive numbers be n, $n + 1$, $n + 2$ and $n + 3$.
  Sum $= n + (n + 1) + (n + 2) + (n + 3)$
     $= 4n + 6$
     $= 2(2n + 3)$
  Since the sum is a multiple of 2, it is always even.
  Therefore the sum of four consecutive numbers is always even.

3 Let the consecutive integers be x, $x + 1$ and $x + 2$.
  Sum of the integers $= x + x + 1 + x + 2 = 3x + 3$
  $= 3(x + 1)$
  As 3 is a factor, the sum must be a multiple of 3.

4 **a** The numerator is larger than the denominator so the fraction will always be greater than 1. Statement is false.
  b As a is larger than b, squaring a will result in a larger number than squaring b. Hence $a^2 > b^2$ so the statement is false.
  c The square root of a number can have two values one positive and the other negative so this statement is false.

Review it! p.61

1 **a** $-9x + 12$ **b** $6x + 4$ **c** $6x^3 + 25x^2 + 16x - 15$

2 **a** $(2x - 1)(x + 4)$ **b** $x = \frac{1}{2}$ or $x = -4$

3 **a** $8x^6y^3$ **b** $6x$ **c** $\frac{5}{b}$

4 $x = 2$, $y = 1$

5 **a** $\frac{3}{x + 7} = \frac{2 - x}{x + 1}$
    $3(x + 1) = (2 - x)(x + 7)$
    $3x + 3 = 2x + 14 - x^2 - 7x$
    $3x + 3 = -x^2 - 5x + 14$
    $x^2 + 8x - 11 = 0$
  b $x = 1.20$ or $x = -9.20$ (to 2 d.p.)

6 $x = \frac{3y - 2z}{az + 1}$

7 **a** $f^{-1}(x) = 3x - 15$ or $f^{-1}(x) = 3(x - 5)$
  b $k = 7$

8 **a** 26, 22, 18 **b** 8th term $= -2$

9 The point lies outside the circle.

10 $x - 9y$

11 **a** $2(x + 2)^2 - 7$
  b **i** $(-2, -7)$
    ii $x = -3.9$ and $x = -0.1$
  c

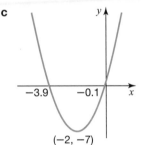

12 30 cm²

13 $y = 7x + 12$

14 $x = -2$, $y = 0$ or $x = \frac{6}{5}$, $y = \frac{8}{5}$

Exam practice answers

Simple algebraic techniques p.64

1 **a** formula   **c** expression **e** formula
  b identity   **d** identity

2 $x + 6x^2$

3 $y^3 - y = (1)^3 - 1 = 0$ so $y = 1$ is correct.
  $y^3 - y = (-1)^3 - (-1) = -1 + 1 = 0$ so $y = -1$ is correct.

4 **a** $10x$ **b** $4x^2 - 6x$ **c** $18x^2$

5 **a** 2   **b** $\frac{7}{8}$ **c** $-\frac{3}{2}$

Removing brackets p.65

1 **a** $24x - 56$ **b** $-6x + 12$

2 **a** $3x + 9$ **c** $10a^2b - 5ab^2$
  b $8xy + 6x - 2y$ **d** $2x^3y^3 + 3x^2y^4$

3 **a** $m^2 + 5m - 24$ **c** $9x^2 - 6x + 1$
  b $8x^2 + 26x - 7$ **d** $6x^2 + xy - y^2$

4 **a** $x^2 + 7x + 10$ **c** $x^2 - 6x - 7$
  b $x^2 - 16$ **d** $15x^2 + 14x + 3$

5 **a** $x^3 + 6x^2 + 5x - 12$ **b** $18x^3 - 63x^2 + 37x + 20$

Factorising p.66

1 **a** $5x(5x - y)$ **b** $2\pi(2r^2 + 3x)$ **c** $6ab^2(a^2 + 2)$

2 **a** $(3x + 1)(3x - 1)$ **b** $4(2x + 1)(2x - 1)$

3 **a** $(a + 4)(a + 8)$ **b** $(p - 6)(p - 4)$

4 **a** $a(a + 12)$ **b** $(b + 3)(b - 3)$ **c** $(x - 5)(x - 6)$

5 **a** $(3x + 8)(x + 4)$ **b** $(3x + 13)(x - 1)$ **c** $(2x - 5)(x + 2)$

6 $\frac{2}{(x - 3)}$ **7** $\frac{2x - 1}{4x + 1}$

Changing the subject of a formula p.68

1 $T = \frac{PV}{nR}$ **3** $a = \frac{v - u}{t}$ **5** $v = \sqrt{\frac{2E}{m}}$

2 $y = \frac{1 - 4x}{2}$ **4** $x = 5(y + m)$

6 **a** $r = \sqrt{\frac{3V}{\pi h}}$ **b** 3.46 cm (to 2 d.p.)

7 **a** $x = \frac{y + 9}{3}$ **b** 4

8 $x = \frac{3y - 2}{a + 1}$

9 **a** $c = \frac{b}{a}$ **b** upper bound for $c = 1.18$ (to 3 s.f.)
               lower bound for $c = 1.11$ (to 3 s.f.)

Solving linear equations p.70

1   **a** $x = 7$ **d** $x = 32$ **g** $x = -2$
   b $x = 5$ **e** $x = 25$ **h** $x = 84$
   c $x = 4$ **f** $x = -9$

2   $x = \frac{2}{3}$

3   **a** $x = \frac{1}{2}$ **b** $x = -\frac{8}{5}$

Solving quadratic equations using factorisation p.71

1   **a** $(x - 3)(x - 4)$ **b** $x = 3$ or $x = 4$
2   **a** $(2x - 1)(x + 3)$ **b** $x = \frac{1}{2}$ or $x = -3$
3   $x = -2$ or $x = 6$
4   **a** $x(x - 8) - 7 = x(5 - x)$ **b** $x = -\frac{1}{2}$ or $x = 7$
      $x^2 - 8x - 7 = 5x - x^2$
      $2x^2 - 13x - 7 = 0$
5   $x = 2\,\text{cm}$

Solving quadratic equations using the formula p.73

1   **a** $\frac{3}{x + 7} = \frac{2 - x}{x + 1}$ **b** $x = 1.20$ or -9.20 (to 2 d.p.)
      $3(x + 1) = (2 - x)(x + 7)$
      $3x + 3 = 2x + 14 - x^2 - 7x$
      $3x + 3 = -x^2 - 5x + 14$
      $x^2 + 8x - 11 = 0$
2   $x = 2.78\,\text{cm}$ (to 2 d.p.)
3   $x = 3.30$ or -0.30 (to 2 d.p.)

Solving simultaneous equations p.74

1   $x = 2$ and $y = 3$

2   **a** 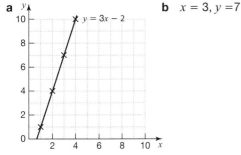   **b** $x = 3$, $y = 7$

3   $x = 0$, $y = -3$ or $x = 3$, $y = 0$

Solving inequalities p.75

1   **a** $x \geq -9$ **b** $x < -12$

2 

3   **a**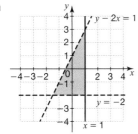

   b $(1, 2)$, $(1, 1)$, $(0, 0)$, $(1, 0)$, $(0, -1)$, $(1, -1)$
4   $-3 \leq x \leq 1$ 5 $x < -3$ and $x > 5$

Problem solving using algebra p.76

1   $42\,\text{m}^2$ 2   cost of adult ticket $= £7.50$
                         cost of child ticket $= £4$

3   **a**   16 years   **b**   9 years

Use of functions p.77

1   **a**   19   **b** $x = -1$
2   **a** $(x - 6)^2$ **b** $x^2 - 6$
3   **a** ± 3 **b** $2x + 5$
4   $f^{-1}(x) = \sqrt{\frac{x - 3}{5}}$

Iterative methods p.78

1   Let $f(x) = 2x^3 - 2x + 1$
   $f(-1) = 2(-1)^3 - 2(-1) + 1 = 1$
   $f(-1.5) = 2(-1.5)^3 - 2(-1.5) + 1 = -2.75$
   There is a sign change of $f(x)$, so there is a solution
   between $x = -1$ and $x = -1.5$.
2   $x_1 = 0.1121111111$
   $x_2 = 0.1125202246$
   $x_3 = 0.1125357073$
3   **a** $x_4 = 1.5213705 \approx 1.521$ (to 3 d.p.)
   b   Checking value of $x^3 - x - 2$ for $x = 1.5205$, 1.5215:
      When $x = 1.5205$ $f(1.5205) = -0.0052$
            $x = 1.5215$ $f(1.5215) = 0.0007$
   Since there is a change of sign, the root is 1.521 correct
   to 3 decimal places.
4   **a**   **i**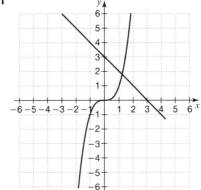

     ii There is a root of $x^3 + x - 3 = 0$ where the graphs
        of $y = x^3$ and $y = 3 - x$ intersect. The graphs
        intersect once so there is one real root of the
        equation $x^3 + x - 3 = 0$.
   b $x_1 = 1.216440399$
      $x_2 = 1.212725591$
      $x_3 = 1.213566964$
      $x_4 = 1.213376503$
      $x_5 = 1.213419623$
      $x_6 = 1.213409861 = 1.2134$ (to 4 d.p.)

Equation of a straight line p.80

1   A
2   **a** $-\frac{4}{3}$ **b** $y = -\frac{1}{2}x + \frac{7}{2}$ **c** $y = 2x + 1$
3   $(3.8, 11.4)$ (to 1 d.p.)

Quadratic graphs p.82

1   **a** $x = -0.3$ or -3.7 (to 1 d.p.)
   b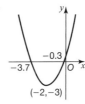

2   $a = 5$, $b = -2$ and $c = -10$
3   $a = 2$, $b = 3$ and $c = -15$

Recognising and sketching graphs of functions p.83

1

Equation	Graph
$y = x^2$	B
$y = 2^x$	D
$y = \sin x°$	E
$y = x^3$	C
$y = x^2 - 6x + 8$	A
$y = \cos x°$	F

2 a

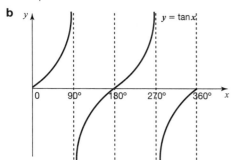

b

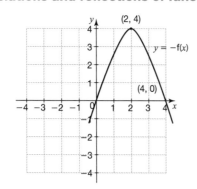

3 $\theta = 70.5°$ or $289.5°$ (to 1 d.p.)

Translations and reflections of functions p.84

1 a

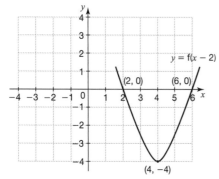

b

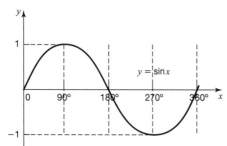

2 a, b, c

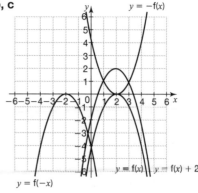

3

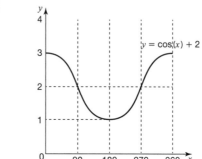

Equation of a circle and tangent to a circle p.85

1 a 5
  b 7
  c 2
2 radius of the circle $= \sqrt{21} = 4.58$
distance of the point $(4, 3)$ from the centre of the circle $(0, 0) = \sqrt{16 + 9} = \sqrt{25} = 5$
This distance is greater than the radius of the circle, so the point lies outside the circle.
3 a $\sqrt{74}$
  b $x^2 + y^2 = 74$ **c** $y = -\frac{5}{7}x + \frac{74}{7}$

Real-life graphs p.86

1 a $1\,\text{m/s}^2$
  b $225\,\text{m}$
2 a The graph is a straight line starting at the origin, so this represents constant acceleration from rest of $\frac{15}{6} = 2.5\,\text{m/s}^2$.
  b The gradient decreases to zero, so the acceleration decreases to zero.
  c $118\,\text{m}$ (to nearest integer); $117\,\text{m}$ is also acceptable
  d It will be a slight underestimate, as the curve is always above the straight lines forming the tops of the trapeziums.

Generating sequences p.87

1 a i $\frac{1}{2}$ **ii** 243   **iii** 21
  b 14, 1
2 $-3, -11$
3 a 25, 36
  b 15, 21
  c 8, 13

The nth term p.88

1 a nth term $= 4n - 2$
  b nth term $= 4n - 2 = 2(2n - 1)$
2 is a factor, so the nth term is divisible by 2 and therefore is even.
  c 236 is not a term in the sequence.

2 **a** 5
   b −391
   c n^2 is always positive, so the largest value $9 - n^2$ can take is 8 when $n = 1$. All values of n above 1 will make $9 - n^2$ smaller than 8. So 10 cannot be a term.

3 nth term $= n^2 - 3n + 3$

Arguments and proofs p.89

1 The only prime number that is not odd is 2, which is the only even prime number.
Hence, statement is false because 2 is a prime number that is not odd.

2 **a** true: $n = 1$ is the smallest positive integer and this would give the smallest value of $2n + 1$ which is 3.
   b true: 3 is a factor of $3(n + 1)$ so $3(n + 1)$ must be a multiple of 3.
   c false: $2n$ is always even and subtracting 3 will give an odd number.

3 Let first number $= x$ so next number $= x + 1$
Sum of consecutive integers $= x + x + 1 = 2x + 1$
Regardless of whether x is odd or even, $2x$ will always be even as it is divisible by 2.
Hence $2x + 1$ will always be odd.

4 $(2x - 1)^2 - (x - 2)^2$
$= 4x^2 - 4x + 1 - (x^2 - 4x + 4)$
$= 4x^2 - 4x + 1 - x^2 + 4x - 4$
$= 3x^2 - 3$
$= 3(x^2 - 1)$
The 3 outside the brackets shows that the result is a multiple of 3 for all integer values of x.

5 Let two consecutive odd numbers be $2n - 1$ and $2n + 1$.
$(2n + 1)^2 - (2n - 1)^2$
$= (4n^2 + 4n + 1) - (4n^2 - 4n + 1)$
$= 8n$
Since 8 is a factor of $8n$, the difference between the squares of two consecutive odd numbers is always a multiple of 8.
(If you used $2n + 1$ and $2n + 3$ for the two consecutive odd numbers, difference of squares $= 8n + 8 = 8(n + 1)$.)

Available at
WHSmith
EST·1792

GCSE Skills

Build confidence with targeted skills practice

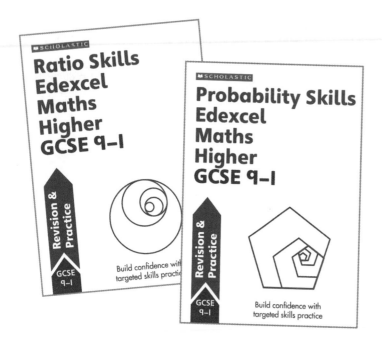

Revise GCSE Maths topics in greater depth

- Clear and focused explanations of tricky topics

- Questions that offer additional challenge

- Deepen understanding and apply knowledge

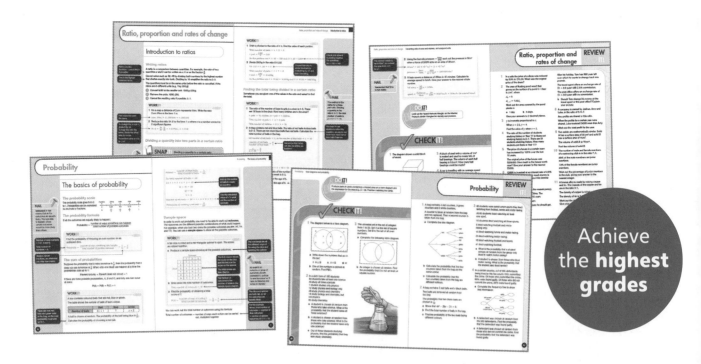

Achieve the **highest grades**

Revision & Practice → **10-Minute Tests** → **National Tests** → **Catch-up & Challenge**

Find out more at **www.scholastic.co.uk/learn-at-home**